THE RISK OF BEING

Michael Gelven

THE
RISK
OF
BEING

What It Means
to
Be Good and Bad

The Pennsylvania State University Press
University Park, Pennsylvania

Library of Congress Cataloging-in-Publication Data

Gelven, Michael.
    The risk of being : what it means to be good and bad / Michael Gelven.
        p.   cm.
    Includes index.
    ISBN 0-271-01707-4 (cloth : alk. paper).
    ISBN 0-271-01708-2 (pbk. : alk. paper).
    1. Good and evil.   2. Philosophical anthropology.   I. Title.
    BJ1406.G45   1997
    170—dc21   96-49104
                                                                  CIP

It is the policy of The Pennsylvania State University Press to use acid-free
paper for the first printing of all clothbound books. Publications on uncoa-
ted stock satisfy the minimum requirements of American National Standard for Information Sciences—Permanence of Paper for Printed Library
Materials, ANSI Z39.48-1992.

To Adam Biesterfeld

Contents

Acknowledgments

In a work such as this, gratitude as well as acknowledgment are due so many more than I can list here. I trust the unmentioned will take no offense at my listing only a few.

I thank Northern Illinios University for the released time associated with my Presidential Research Professorship, and the staff of the Philosophy Department for all the clerical assistance that went far beyond job descriptions. Special thanks to Dr. Herman Stark for reading and criticizing the manuscript, and similar thanks to my sister, Dr. Fran Mayeski, for her comments. For contributions given in lengthy conversations, my thanks to Sharon Sytsma, Donald Livingston, Frank Gonzalez, Troy Cross, and David Billings. A special thanks to those of my students whose eagerness to learn caused me to dig more deeply and strive to make thorny issues untangled and muddy ideas clear.

Part One

Locating the Question

Prelude

Raising the Question

There is something missing in our approach to ethics. Few philosophical disciplines frustrate as deeply as the crucial inquiry into good and bad. Just as a so-called story without a plot leaves the reader curiously dissatisfied, so the formal and critical accounts of moral principles and ethical definitions, even when brilliantly done, leave us disarmed where most we need their wisdom. This sense of frustration, or even being cheated, is not due to any lack of profundity given the received questions by giants in the canon. Plato, Aristotle, Aquinas, Hume, and Kant are deservedly the masters of our apprenticeship; indeed, our frustration stems in part from the remarkable soundness of their analyses. The quarrel is not with how well they have performed but is that, in responding favorably to their labor, there remains a stark realization of what is left unconsidered. What is missing in the traditional approaches might be called the reality of being good and bad. We seem to want to know what it means to *be* good and bad, not merely to discover the principles that govern or should govern our conduct, nor even to precise our definitions of ethical concepts, but to learn what it is *like* to be good and bad.

The phrase, "being like," however, is a colloquial locution, and may seem out of place in a philosophical inquiry. Perhaps, however, this phrase deserves reflection rather than dismissal precisely because it seems to draw our attention to a legitimate question that may be unreachable by the more formal and received vocabulary. A young man considering the approach of an awesome institution may ask his elder brother, "What is it like being married?" He asks neither for the legal definition, nor his duties, obligations, and rights inherent in the institution, although they obviously play some role in the response. He is not asking merely for the personal feelings or the psychological state that follow the ceremony. If the brother has some sensitivity and insight, and if he takes the question seriously and with affection for the one who asks it, we can imagine the kinds of replies that might serve as a meaningful response. They may be couched in autobiographical and personal terms of the elder brother's experience, but this particularity need not forfeit their universality or authority. He may tell of a quarrel that, though heated, seems to be possible just because the security of the sacrament assures both husband and wife that their momentary anger cannot undermine what binds them together; or he might tell of the secret unexpected joy he finds in her own triumphs, or the curious dread when he realizes the absolute obligation he owes her even beyond his love. He may even tell of the awesome wonder and chilling duty at the coming of his first child. These are concrete, direct, and yet enlightening accounts that help the younger brother appreciate the reality of his forthcoming state.

To ask what it is "like" to be good and bad is an indirect, colloquial way to ask what it means to be good and bad—that is, to ask about the reality of being good and bad. The analogy with marriage is meant first to show us that there can be legitimate questions that purely formal considerations may not answer; but it also suggests that such questions may indeed be fundamental. For the institutional aspects of marriage exist just because of these concrete realities. We do not love our spouses, commit ourselves to them, and have children because of marriage; rather, marriage is established because of the reality of love, fidelity, and family. In the same way we do not discover the reality of our being good and bad because there are principles; rather, we elicit the principles because we are already good and bad. It is the reality that grounds the institutions, and because this is so the questions about what it means to be real in these ways is fundamental.

It would never occur to us to raise ethical questions at all if we were not first already both good and bad, and since the reality of our being good and bad precedes the analytic concerns of the principles that govern our conduct, any inquiry focusing primarily on such concerns must fail in some way to provide direct access to how we understand our ethical reality. What does it mean to speak this way? What is "ethical" (or "moral") reality? And how can we approach this reality philosophically?

The suggestion implicit in this question is that our reality itself is somehow dependent on the conjunction of these fundamental notions: Our being good and bad constitutes who we are and what it means for us to be at all. These notions are thus not mere possibilities or disjunctive predicates. We do not say we can be good *or* bad, as we say we can be fat or thin, hungry or sated. For if I am hungry, then I am not sated, although time may alter the ascription of these conflicting properties. But we can say we are both good *and* bad, and mean by this not that we are sometimes one and sometimes the other but that being both is essential for being who we are. We are, therefore, in our reality, finite; and in *this* sense of finite we mean the confrontation of our own being good and bad as a persistent, necessary conflict within ourselves. This conflict is an essential part of our reality; perhaps in some sense the conflict simply is our reality. If this is so, we want to know how we both think and feel about it. There must be a felt *pathos* in both being good and in being bad; and there must be a *logos* or authoritative way of thinking about what it means to be in this conflict. (Chapters 12 and 13, on both the pathos and the logos, respectively, of being good and bad occur near the end of this inquiry, followed by Chapter 14, on the reality of being good and bad.) But such necessary reflections are entirely lacking in the traditional accounts of ethics and morality.

It is necessary, then, first to consider the various stages of how we think about these issues in order to set the boundaries between traditional questions and the unique inquiry that stands out as heretofore relatively unconsidered.

Given a catechism that lists the prohibitions and duties, we recognize that philosophical reflection is not satisfied even if we provisionally accept these precepts on our conduct. For we do not begin with an ethical tabula rasa, wondering if we should be cruel to children or treacherous to those we owe loyalty or murderous of our parents. We already know these are things we ought not to do; these prescriptions bind prior to the philosopher's inquiry. Accepting them, we may seek their inherent rules or maxims to help us resolve conflicts within these prescriptive lists, but such seeking is merely for the sake of easing the anguish of indecision when the hesitant cannot be endured. We may even succeed in isolating principles and hence in refining judgments; we may further make precise the definitions of good and bad so that meaningful disputation may take place. And we may take no little satisfaction in these worthy accomplishments simply because of their truth, since it is truth for its own sake that guides all philosophical passion. But it is truth for its own sake that also prompts us to be dissatisfied with these endeavors, for they do not provide the whole truth.

The ethical prescriptions and descriptions may further lead us beyond the strictly ethical into metaphysical speculation. What makes us good or bad? We learn about the will and the various lures that may attract it. If however there are lures outside the will that make it good or bad, then the will is merely a neurological central-exchange, in which the calls from the moral law are good and those from the baser instincts are bad. But this explanation simply explains away what matters, or puts it on a higher, unreachable shelf. The instantiation of the will as a metaphysical mechanism is a placebo, for we know it is not our wills that do what is right or what is wrong; rather *we* do these things, and because we do them, who we are matters, and it is this mattering that is left out in the traditional accounts.

But if neither critically refined prescriptive lists, nor precise definitions of terms, nor metaphysical speculation on the faculties that allow us to be moral agents entirely satisfy, then what questions remain? We ask not what is The Good, as if seeking a definition; or what ought we to do, as if asking for the proper prescriptions; or even asking how we can act at all, exploring the nature of the will; but rather: What does it *mean to be* good and bad? This is at least a different question than the others. And it may be the fundamental question, the one that addresses our reality as being good and bad.

If this question is to satisfy, two dangers must be preempted. It must first be clear that the question is truly distinct from those raised in the traditional approach to ethics; and it must also be clear that the question is philosophically legitimate, that it is not a matter merely of how one feels or what one believes, but that what it means to be good and bad is a universal question, permitting of an authoritative response. Both of these tasks are formidable but the first is the more daunting, for to try to convince the learned that the question is unique and original, that it is even possible to ask in a way that has not been tried before, seems to offend by arrogance. What, you ask, does it mean to be good? We already have an honored reservoir of tried and familiar answers. Aristotle argues that to be good is to be happy; Plato, that it is to excel at our nature; Kant, that it is to obey the moral law; Aquinas, that it is to please God. Why, then, is this a new question if it already has ancient answers? But such responses, profound as they are in their own right, do not connect at all with the question; for we are not asking what other things we must do to become good, or how to evaluate lives or actions as good, or how to reduce good to another term. The emphasis of this question is on the infinitive: What does it mean *to be* good; and questions raised infinitively must be answered in the same way. We do not answer the question What does it mean to be in jail? by providing a description of the jailhouse or by listing the crimes that bring us there. We respond in kind by showing what it means to be denied our liberty or to be judged as criminal or to be lonely and afraid. To ask what it means to be good and bad is to ask an existential-ontological question. Because the infinitive is unanchored to any specific subject it entails a universality, and with it a rational authority that saves it from personal autobiography or relativism. And so the question is distinct, originary, and for the most part not considered directly by traditional thinkers. Yet, the wise have not been entirely unaware of it, for much of what these great figures say can and does throw light upon this question, just as the architecture of the jail does not fail to hint indirectly at what it means to be in there. It is the indirection that misleads; why not ask it directly?

But how can we to ask this question directly? What kind of responses can be expected? What are the phenomena that ground this question in the concrete? This last formulation is revealing, for we must resist the tendency to respond with mere speculation. There *are* phenomena that we confront that compel this unique and ranking question to be considered directly. The concreteness of these phenomena gives the inquiry a satisfyingly experiential basis even as it retains its a priori authority; it also provides a hint as to how to structure this inquiry.

There are two distinct kinds of phenomena that make available an authoritative reflection on what it means to be real as good and bad. The first kind are those that make us directly aware of the inner conflict itself; the second are those that provide us with actual ways of being bad, that when confronted directly provide us with concrete ways of being good. We may call the first kind "provoking" because in them we are forced by an existential provocation, which is almost always negative and painful, to realize that we are indeed in conflict with ourselves. We can call the second kind "reflective" because as concrete phenomena they nevertheless show us exactly how these conflicts reveal what it means to be bad, and in resistance to them, what it means to be good. To begin with negative confrontations follows from the realization that our reality itself is conflictive: We exist as good and bad.

The Provoking Phenomena

There are two of these: reprimand and outrage. We begin the discovery of our own reality precisely when our natural instincts are checked. There is a violence done to our unreflective and instinctive impulse to gratify ourselves. The parental reprimand that frustrates forces us to become aware of who we are as somehow possessing conflicting maxims within ourselves. Even though many of these reprimands may be entirely absorbed as simply prudential engineering they nevertheless awaken a sense that the negative—being denied—is a fundamental part of us. "Do not touch the hot stove" may be a parental command or even an inner maxim based on painful experience, but it negatively checks a primary curiosity. What it means to be reprimanded, therefore, has powerful existential significance, which is explored in Chapter 1. But its phenomenal immediacy is a given, and reveals itself as fundamental to our own reality. Whatever else we are, we can be pulled up and checked by reprimand, either from others or ourselves. This opens the crack of reflection.

The second provoking phenomenon is outrage, discussed in the second half of Chapter 1. Outrage forces us to face—and hence to *feel*—the reality of unanswered wrong—to *think* in terms of justice and injustice. In outrage the wrong is not merely conceptual or abstract, but directly felt. Yet *as* wrong it is not a mere subjective emotion, captive in a private cage of personal history lacking authority or universality. Indeed, the bitter poignancy of outrage lies precisely in the inescapable realization that a wrong unanswered— injustice—compels because of its transcendence beyond personal feeling. To be outraged inevitably confronts us again with our finitude, for in this phenomenon we are faced with an irretrievable loss of what is precious. It is because we cannot restore the life of the murdered innocent, or the reputation of the scandalized, or the trust of a violated loyalty, that outrage, while demanding redress, cannot be equalized by it. The phenomenon cruelly provokes the confrontation with what it means to be impotent even as it impresses an urgency to respond. In outrage we are in conflict with ourselves, and to *feel* this conflict is thus to be made aware forcefully of our truth. We learn who we are.

These two provoking phenomena, reprimand and outrage, make us aware of ourselves as fundamentally conflictive, and thus reflect the grounding insight that we are not merely capable of doing right *or* wrong, but are essentially already (a priori) good *and* bad.

The Reflective Phenomena

There are three of these: folly-judgment, temptation-courage, and corruption-character. Folly, temptation, and corruption, as phenomena, reveal the three ways of being bad. When confronted, the counter-phenomena are judgment, courage, and character, which are the three ways of being good. The analyses of these three pathoempirical phenomena make up the bulk of Chapters 2 through 9, and to adumbrate this analysis here would distract from the approach. It is enough to point out that these reflective phenomena that constitute the existential basis of what it means to be good and bad are palpably conflictive. We first must be finite in our knowledge, and hence necessarily foolish (but not necessarily *silly*), before we can be wise—that is, before we are able to make judgments. There is no courage unless there is the allure to temptation (the greatest of which may well be fear); and unless we tend to lose our integrity in corruption we cannot have character. This may seem to suggest that we are first fundamentally bad and then only in rejection of our basic nature can we become good; but this must be rejected. Prior to the awareness of our inner conflicts, however, we are not naturally good but merely innocent, which means being unable to be good or bad due to an immature ignorance of our reality. (It is because of this innocent ignorance that folly and judgment are the initial reflective phenomena to compel our attention.) The priority of the negative is philosophically or methodologically first because of the need to establish the immediacy of the provoking phenomena; neither good nor bad has metaphysical priority because our reality is conflictive; hence, they are interdependent notions. It is therefore proper to speak of the three, rather than the six, reflective phenomena, though in the analysis they are placed under six different headings.

What is the nature of this analysis? Throughout the course of this inquiry there emerges a synthesizing argumentation that rests on three pillars, themselves discovered or uncovered only through the unfolding journey. The first is that the existential methodology is prior to any specific moral or ethical analysis. This is a formal point and is made available only in following out the inquiry. The second pillar is the very real distinction between morality and ethics. The former concerns itself with what we ought to do, the latter with living a good life. It is only in light of this distinction that a good person can do a bad thing, a surprisingly fertile truth that yields an ample harvest of reflection. If morality and ethics are distinct, then neither one is sufficient in itself for being good; however, even to conjoin them requires a synthesizing and prior authority, which shows even more concretely that only the present question about what it means to be good is wide enough to fuse together what is divided. The third pillar is that we are not good *or* bad, but good *and* bad—which does not mean we must *do* what is good as well as what is bad, but that the fundamental presupposition for responsibility and moral ascription lies in our *being* good *and* bad fundamentally. But this shift from "or" to "and" has remarkable consequences that emerge in the course of these reflections, not the least of which is the realization that only by already being both good and bad can it matter to do what is right rather than what is wrong.

What is missing in the traditional approach to ethics is therefore revealed as the existentially concrete underpinning that confronts these denuding phenomena as the actual arenas of our struggles. This is not merely to insist that psychological feelings be added to formal principles as sauce is added to meat, for it is rather these confrontations themselves that are the meat to which the sauces of reflection and analysis are added to reveal their truth. But even if this is accepted provisionally, what is the proper philosophical procedure?

I invite the reader simply to plunge directly into the torrent of the inquiry, mapless and unguided, enjoying the trek for whatever it uncovers, as an adventure. Sketching out the milestones of the journey, and even foretelling the destination, seems to transform what would be an inquiry into a treatise. The text is not meant to provide a series of logical supports for a thesis outlined in advance, as if in medieval fashion a certain claim is presented to be demonstrated by rational critique. The spirit of the work is closer to a Platonic dialogue or to the ruminations of later Heidegger. It is a reflective meditation, inviting the reader along on a journey of discovery. There is no engaging in scholarly quarrels, no pitting of one thesis against its counterthesis, no debate between established traditions. Such techniques are honorable and in certain contexts necessary, but they are not the only methodologies for approaching philosophical truth. There is no doubt that much of what is in this text has relevance to prior disputation, and that it is possible on various occasions to direct the readers' attention to these precedents, thereby satisfying the academic passion for footnotes and pigeonholes. If I forgo this etiquette it is not merely to irritate—and certainly not to assume originality—in the face of greater precedent genius. It is rather to avoid distraction from the *adventure* of learning.

1

Provoking Phenomena

Reprimand

Perhaps it is because laws, by their very nature, must prohibit certain actions; perhaps it is because when we were very young our parents punished us for doing certain things, and called us good when we did not; perhaps it is because the commandments that we remember demand that we shalt not—for whatever reason, there is a proclivity to think about what is good in negative terms. Good, like cold, is an absence. List the prohibited acts, avoid doing them, and goodness follows like air rushing into a vacuum. Goodness is simply what is left over when the bad is cleaned away. It is the floor on which the bad dirt falls and that, when swept, becomes clean and good again.

It is difficult to shake off this obviously naive and misleading persuasion that would canonize, were it fully pressed, bovine stupor and placid equanimity as ultimate achievements of the human spirit. Philosophy is by no means lacking positive theories of what is good. For the classical Greeks, goodness is the achievement of happiness, which is certainly positive. Even hedonism has the advantage that pleasure is more than a mere absence of pain. Saint Augustine argues that goodness consists in the love of God, and all good actions follow from this primary motivation. Kant assures us that acting out of respect for the moral law is to treat all rational beings as ends. In the speculative realm, therefore, the notion of goodness as a negation of badness has little if any status whatsoever. And yet, it is precisely this noncorrespondence with the naive view that renders such speculations lacking or incomplete. These great thinkers obviously have contributed much to our understanding, but if an original and fundamental inquiry into what it means to be good is to be deeply rooted in the way we actually think about the issue, the point of departure, even though it be naive or possibly fundamental, must somehow account for these instincts to see goodness, if not merely as the opposite of the bad, at least as some kind of response to it.

For there can be no doubt that we are far more aware of what it means to be bad than to be good, and this is unsettling and even disturbing. We have little difficulty in spotting bad people: Hitler and Stalin were bad because of the great suffering they caused so many; and the list of those we call bad far exceeds those we call good. To be sure, we also seem to know who is good: Mother Teresa, a rare example in these contemporary days when saints are forgotten, helps those who are afflicted, and she is honored as goodly. But even she seems a precarious model, for her very goodness is seen in terms of what she does to alleviate what is bad. Were social engineering to be refined to the point where poverty, crime, injustice, and disease were eradicated, even Mother Teresa would seem to fade as paragon, for unless there are great ills to battle and great suffering to succor, we would not know her at all. The implication seems to be that evil is a positive thing like pain, and good is merely the denial of it. The greatest good, then, would be nothing more than the most effective anesthetic. If the world were entirely devoid of all misery, would this mean that all would be good? or, would saints cry out that their opportunity for goodness would vanish if the ills and wrongs of the world were to vanish first? If no one were wronged, would justice be possible? Were there no great difficulties to overcome, would courage disappear? If lies were not told, would honesty cease to matter? Or do we actually mean by justice merely rectifying injustice, by courage merely overcoming cowardice, by honesty overcoming deceit? If so, then virtue depends on vice; the good is merely the absence of the bad, and avoiding wrong is the only right.

Even that triumph of human excellence, love, seems of value only if not distorted by excess; for love is the sire to jealousy; it is the lure that leads us to adulterous violation of marital oaths or to the wanton profligacy of hedonism, or the ignoble hegemony of enslaving passion. Even in love, it seems, to be good is nothing else but the avoidance of being bad. If, in order to be good, I wish to help others in their distress, then it seems I must want others to *be* in distress, simply so I can help them. But if I truly wish no one were in distress, and doing good requires my beneficence, then in wanting all to be good I cannot *be* good. It was W. H. Auden, I believe, who, when asked what the purpose of life is, responded that he was put on earth to help others; but what the others are here for he had no idea.

But surely these are outrageous suggestions. Good must be more than avoiding bad; there must be something positive, something independent of vice or evil, about being good. To suggest that what it means to be good is *merely* not being bad is to suggest that in the absence of bad good has no meaning on its own. Health is meaningful without disease; a perfectly healthy child need not be fighting against cancer in order to be judged healthy. There are positive criteria that can be listed that identify health; disease is seen as the absence of one or more of these criteria, making disease the negation of the positive health. And so it would seem that goodness, like health, should have positive and not merely negative meaning. Furthermore, there is the danger of defining correlatives solely in terms of the negation of their opposites: health is the absence of disease, but disease is the absence of health; good is the absence of bad, but bad is the absence of good. Such circularity is frustrating, silly, and misological.

Nevertheless, the problem inherent in finding what it means to be good other than as a negation of being bad persists. Few would deny the correlation between the two; just as health and disease are correlatives. But there seems no ready resource for understanding what it means to be good beyond that of negating the bad. Even in the arts the bad is more easily represented. The great novelist Fyodor Dostoyevsky succeeds far more in his depiction of Roskolnikoff in *Crime and Punishment* than in the depiction of the saintly Prince Mishkin in *The Idiot.* Goodness always seems to require some great struggle against evil in order to be artistically represented with any degree of success; indeed, in those artworks that do accomplish a meaningful sense of goodness, it is always as a triumph over wickedness; goodness by itself is simply uninteresting, even dull—which is a morally repugnant notion that is fundamentally unacceptable.

Perhaps one reason why the question What does it mean to be good? is so elusive is that no one we know is perfectly good. A child can be perfectly healthy, but not perfectly good, for in order to be good he must confront his own badness. The child as innocent, is not *capable* of being good, lacking this confrontation. On the other hand, to confront one's badness means one is not perfectly good, for the badness within us that we must confront already diminishes our goodness. Thus there is no possible model to revere as perfectly good.

This shift from the term "absence" to the term "confront" is by no means insignificant; it shows us that whatever it means to be good cannot be made intelligible solely in terms of negation, for it is not the mere *absence* of bad, but the confronting and overcoming of it that makes us good. Whatever makes it *possible* to overcome or to confront what is bad in us is, at the very least, not merely an absence or a negation, the way poverty can be seen as a mere absence of wealth. It is, of course, tempting to speculate on what makes this confrontation possible, whether it be a faculty like a free will or a conditioning like a virtue, or a more fundamental given, like character. But such metaphysical speculation is retrograde to the method of this inquiry, and the temptation to indulge in it now must be resisted.

It is enough to realize that what it means to be good must include as a part of its meaning that the bad be confronted or checked, as in a reprimand. "Johnny, stop hurting your little sister!" The child hears in this reprimand a check on his primitive instincts for self-indulgence. But this parental censure, as reprimand, not only restricts behavior but also provokes a realization of a conflicting concern that may even be (and probably should be) articulated: "You should be ashamed of yourself. Consider *her* feelings!" There is pain in having to disappoint his instinct for superiority through intimidation and violence, but there is also a realization, through his parent's concern, that his sister, too, matters. This provokes a conflict: his desires for mastery matters but so does his parents' concern for his sister, which may eventually produce even his own concern for her. But if *she* matters, and his primitive instincts also matter, he is suddenly aware that being good is conflictive. Being good must therefore have some positive power, since conflicts are always and only between powers. But with this realization, being good is not reducible to or equated with the mere *absence* of being bad but recognized in the conflict as an authority in its own right, although always in terms of the conflict. It is the conflict that gives legitimacy and hence autonomy to being good, so that goodness independent of the conflict is a pure abstraction. Even as abstract, however, it is epistemically correlative to being bad—which is simply to say I cannot understand the one without the other. Furthermore, to suggest that to be good necessarily entails a confrontation with being bad opens a rich treasury of methodological approaches: If to confront what is bad necessarily means to have some positive characteristic that makes such confrontation possible, then we have already found a way to carry out this inquiry. By examining the very confrontations themselves some indication should be made available that would allow us to trace them back to their origin and thus open up an access to the question of what it means to be good.

If what it means to be good consists, in part at least, of overcoming or confronting what is bad, then goodness cannot be reduced to mere placidity or vacuity. What it means to be good now becomes genuinely interesting; we are not left with the good as spineless vapidity.

But although this may seem a simple truth, it has great significance. If being good were merely avoiding bad, the placid would be our saints. It is the consequent that appalls us; and so by modus tollens we deny the antecedent. But why abjure the consequent? What is it that offends us in this equation of the placid with the good?

Outrage

Seeing his beloved friend lying murdered at the base of Pompey's statue, Mark Antony questions his own seeming placidity:

> That I did love thee Caesar, O! 'tis true:
> If then thy spirit look upon us now,
> Shall it not grieve thee dearer than thy death
> To see thy Antony making his peace,
> Shaking the bloody fingers of thy foes . . . .

For what does it mean to be a friend and then shake the hands of the friend's assassins? It seems a friendship means nothing at all. To wink at a friend's murder is to condone it. Might it not be a necessary condition of loving a friend that his death would stir us to outrage? Indeed, shortly after the conspirators leave him alone with the body, Antony expresses exactly this sentiment:

> Oh! pardon me, thou bleeding piece of earth,
> That I am meek and gentle with these butchers; . . .

He then takes an oath that, to avenge this wrong, he will visit on all Italy such "domestic fury and fierce civil strife" that "mothers shall but smile when they behold / Their infants quartered with the hands of war . . ." It is a dreadful, if magnificent, promise and it shows us what true outrage means. Outrage is a confrontation with a wrong. Perhaps then, by probing into what it means, we can understand something about overcoming this wrong. Were there no outrage, the rank injustice would be without offense; and without offense there is no redress, without which there is no justice whatsoever. So it is the outrage that reveals the wrongness of the wrong, and as a confrontation it makes possible the righting of the wrong—which is part of what it means to be good. And so outrage demands philosophical examination. But this citation from a great drama requires some caution in its analysis, for it is not outrage as a psychological state but as a dramatic disclosure of truth that matters. We do not ask what it means for Antony to feel outrage but what his outrage reveals to us, the audience. And surely the first dramatic impact of these moving words is our realization of how precious and dear Caesar was and how that preciousness, by his murder, has been forfeit; yet only as forfeit, can it achieve its truth. The precious is very often revealed only by its loss. And this great truth can be illumined by unpacking the dramatist's *craft*. For in the first two acts, Caesar is presented to us in less than glowing terms. We see him not greatly but through the eyes of his enemies, especially Cassius. And even when Caesar himself speaks, there is always that ironic touch that exposes his fallibility.

> I rather tell thee what is to be fear'd
> Than what I fear, for always I am Caesar.
> Come on my right hand, for this ear is deaf . . .

After so great a line as "for always I am Caesar" follows the startling, denuding admission that his left ear is deaf! A flaw, so common as to be base, in so noble a being as he, clues the audience that the mighty are vulnerable. Caesar appears majestic only seconds before the murder when we glimpse at his greatness in the comparison of himself to the Northern Star, unmoved as others are by base spaniel fawning. But Caesar dead, eulogized by an outraged Antony, offers more than a glimpse; it teaches us the greater truth. However flawed he may have been—however dangerous to the Republic—in Antony's splendid outrage alone do we confront the true meaning of this regicide: the absolutely irreplaceable, the supremely precious, has been basely removed—and for a political reason.

This is the very soul of outrage: the sense of loss; the dread awareness that, bereft of greatness, we ourselves are diminished. Even were Caesar deserving of his slaughter, as he well may have been, his murder remains, in Brutus' words, a "savage spectacle." For it is the outrage of his loss that depicts what it means for there to have been, however fleeting, magnificence. But magnificence being lost, particularly through murderous larceny, cannot be borne with equanimity.

In addition to verifying the precious in its loss, the power of outrage stuns us with denuding impotence. There is nothing we can do to restore what has been usurped. Outrage is therefore not only against the loss but against our own shrunken incapacity to regain it. There is a dreadful confrontation with our own finitude, a mocking of our ability to measure up to the enormity of the loss and its implications. This impotence is profoundly denuding, for we are, in its thrall, entirely disarmed by the irretrievable. Outrage does not occur when a loss is merely possible, but only when it is absolute. We are often stunned by the unredeemable—the full realization that certain things, like death or an unguarded insult that wounds forever, cannot be retrieved. In this way, outrage becomes a kind of desperate helplessness, like a mother watching her child die, which savages our milky limitation into a self-loathing that cannot be comforted. When the splendid leaks through our hands like water, we hate our own unwebbed fingers for being too porous to hold the precious liquid. This suggests that outrage is not only, or even chiefly, against a perpetrator but against ourselves. It is as if, because we are impotent, we never deserved to have had the precious in the first place and, realizing this, it seems an impudence to have thought we did.

The impotence in outrage, however, is not entirely feckless. Some deep, sequestered, hitherto unspotted origin sires in this fell realization of absolute loss, a most curious birthing.

Something stirs deep within us and waxes quickly, thrusting out of our impotence a denial of all quiescence: a howling. To howl is to forge wordless speech, but it is no less significant for this. In outrage, stunned to a self-loathing impotence, we seek to redress this nudity in formless speech. If we can do nothing to undo the wrong, we at least must howl to undo the silence that condones the wrong. The metaphors of speech seem inherent in Antony's outrage:

> Over the wounds now do I prophecy,
> Which like dumb mouths do ope their ruby lips.
> To beg the voice and utterance of my tongue.

We seek redress of our impotent nudity in language—even if it is only the preverbal language of howling. We are impelled to howl; and if sustained, we bring the howl to speech, a speech by which we speak *against* as in a curse. "A curse shall light upon the limbs of men." But in this translation from howl to curse we note a curious alteration in the power of language. For a curse is not mere words but a deliberate willing of dreadful consequence. To curse is to empower language to darken the future. We do not need to believe in the theological machinery that accounts for how this happens: A curse, like a promise, does not depend upon its success to be meaningful. To promise is to commit to future action that, if unfulfilled, removes neither obligation nor the meaning of the promise as future-determining. So a curse is still a curse even if there are no gods or devils to carry it out. In Antony's case, the curse is itself a prophecy that is within his power to realize. Yet a curse is not a mere promise to avenge. It calls upon the powers that transcend normal dealings; it is to enter into that curious realm of language in which, like blessing, the sacred is intoned. Outrage, therefore, prevails upon language to transcend the ordinary; in the howl of outrage the ordinary is shouted down. We no longer appeal to common feelings or common powers. The wrong is not a mere moral blight but a sacrilege. Caesar murdered becomes Caesar martyred; he is no longer a mere wronged mortal but an outrage before the heavens. Thus, the title of the play does not refer to the character (who after all says very little in the first two acts and is dead and gone by the middle of the third) but to the *problem* of "Julius Caesar." Caesar unavenged insults both justice and Rome itself; but avenged, both Rome and justice are savaged by civil war. Antony's outrage calls down a curse upon all of his countrymen, thereby revealing the power of language to evoke the sacred. In this way, outrage is revealed as a child of language; only speakers can be outraged.

A curse is of the same linguistic modality as a prayer or a blessing—but it is not a prayer, else we could not curse God. It is rather a transcendent call to language itself, to accomplish what we as impotent and bereft of the precious cannot. This appeal is not idle superstition; no less a philosophical genius than Immanuel Kant argues that our own finite inability to achieve justice in this life prompts the mind to postulate immortality. I cannot will a world with unanswered wrongs, and so I must will a divine retributor. But cursing is not an argument—it is the linguistic expression of the phenomenon of outrage.

It must be clearly stated that outrage is neither a desire for justice nor a moral imperative demanding specific action. There may indeed be a moral or ethical response when faced with unanswered wrong that would compel us to punish the offender. Perhaps it may even be argued that, morally, one is obligated to redress all offenses if possible, but such considerations, although entirely legitimate, do not belong in this reflection on outrage. For it is the very essence of outrage that reveals our impotence even as it exposes how dear and precious was whatever we have lost. These twin revelations result in an unexpected power in our language, the power to curse. These discoveries are about who we are. The need for redress is undoubtedly a part of this phenomenon—this need is the basis of our discovered impotence—but the phenomenon as such cannot provide any moral imperative or any ethical principle. Furthermore, it is absolutely essential in this present inquiry to quarantine all moral or ethical commands because we learn from these discoveries that moral imperatives and ethical concerns are *derived;* that what is fundamental is the question, what it means to be good. Hence to focus on moral principles as the *beginning* of ethical inquiry is to distract from the more fundamental truth. The phenomenon of outrage is here being examined solely to cast some early light on what it means to be good.

A few preparatory gleams have been isolated. At the very least we have discovered that to confront the bad in the phenomenon of outrage is to denude our finitude and endure the irretrievable. This points to the fundamental realization that to be good must stem from our finitude; to be good is to be able to hold something or someone dear, and to be able, in the curse, to call upon the sacred. It also suggests that to be able to be good requires the capacity to suffer and to endure a loss so precious that in confronting it we must seek redress.

But these discoveries are only of indications or pointers. They are not to be trivialized but neither are they to be ranked as satisfying. We do not learn from this how to achieve justice or even what justice is fundamentally. But we do learn that, to be good, justice matters. And what makes it matter is our being good, not the other way around. For the discovery of the precious, the learning of our finitude, the origin of our cursing, all stem from who we are. What we do, or even ought to do, follows from this. Being capable of outrage presupposes that the loss of the precious and the consequent impotence that evokes a curse *matter.*

As slender as this may seem, it is nevertheless a fundamental discovery, for it is a complete reversal of the opening lines of the previous section that implied being good was merely a neutral condition intelligible only as the negative pole of the correlative, bad. There must be a way or ways from which we can gather sufficient resistance to counter the influences that we call bad, and this strength or power to resist is being good. But how are we to understand this goodness? Perhaps the method just utilized can be extended. By reflecting on the different ways we think about being bad, it may be possible, in countering these, to discover the different ways we think about being good. How do we react to our own being bad?

"How could I have been so stupid?" When we say this we seem to be aghast at our own ignorance, although we do not, by the expostulation, seek excuse in our ignorance. And so the ghastly reaction to our own nonexcusatory ignorance or folly offers the first line of inquiry. But it is not the only reaction we make.

"Why did I not resist this wrong?" When we cry out in this way we express shame at our own weakness. Thus a second line of inquiry offers itself in the reflection on what it means to be weak and why we are ashamed of it.

"What have I let myself become?" is a third, and probably the most damning, of all self-indictments, which, when unpacked philosophically, may reveal how and why our own character can be abhorrent to us.

Each of these three reactions to our own being bad may, by a kind of moral modus tollens, serve as a concrete source of reflection by which we may discover, in part at least, what it means to be good.

Part Two

What It Means to Be Bad

2

The Three Ways to Be Bad

Ghastly Ignorance

"How could I have been so stupid?"

We do not hold responsible those whose ignorance entirely miti-gates censure. The innocent passenger who pushes the elevator button, unaware of the children playing in the shaft, is ignorant but not bad. On the other hand, the truckdriver who backs his rig into the street without looking may be ignorant of the children playing on the sidewalk; but since we consider normal precaution to be a part of responsible driving, we say he is criminally negligent and deserves harsh penalties from the law. Neither of these kinds of ignorance are of interest here—the first because there is no cul-pability at all; the second because the culpability is due to care-lessness and a failure of responsibility, and the ignorance is inci-dental. He *ought* to have known.

But there is a third kind of ignorance that seems to generate censure *as* ignorance. How is this possible? Does not ignorance always excuse, or at least mitigate? How can I be held respon-sible for what I do not *know*? We must be very careful in walk-ing through this ethical minefield, bearing in mind that the sole interest of this inquiry is the confrontation of what it means to be ignorant in such a way as to evoke the response of being aghast.

Emilia, aghast at what Othello has done to Desdemona is magnificent in her reproach: "O gull! O dolt! / As ignorant as dirt!" And later in that same, final act, the Moor accepts this charge, asking that they speak of

> . . . one whose hand,
> Like the base Indian, threw a pearl away,
> Richer than all his tribe . . .

In what way is Othello "ignorant as dirt"? And why are we, the audience, aghast? If he is truly like the base Indian, who in ignorance throws away a pearl, should we not rather extenuate and be sad rather than aghast? But Othello entreats them:

> When you shall these unlucky deeds relate,
> Speak of me as I am; nothing extenuate . . .

And so he himself will not take refuge in the ignorance that excuses. How are we to understand this?

The ignorance that is ghastly, that is like dirt, that is bad, is the ignorance in bad judgment. It is the ignorance that is closer to the originary verb—it ignores. Othello has judged both Desdemona and Iago badly, and to retreat behind an excusatory cloak is to deny that his judgment is essential for being who he is.

To judge is not the same as to know, yet neither is it simple guessing or arbitrary prejudice. One who judges a gymnast's performance may not be able to account for his assessment in terms of absolute decision procedures, but it is not entirely subjective or biased for this lack. There need not be any vagueness, for the judgment that Michelangelo's *David* is a magnificent artwork is not vague at all. When a general judges the situation on the battlefield as ripe for splitting his forces, it may well be that not one of his majors or colonels could distinguish, as he does, precisely the right moment. The facts are there, and both general and colonel see exactly the same thing. But one reads the picture more wisely, which is why the general wears the stars on his shoulder. If he reads it badly, his judgment goes down in history as a bad one and we are aghast at his failure. Judgment, therefore, is not the possession of mere information, though information (distorted pompously by technology to "data") may well play a role in it. Rather, to judge is to measure, weigh, compare, test, and assess what is known. There are those who see clouds of dust on the horizon; and those who see the clouds as a flanking move of the enemy. There are those who see a group of women and children on the French shore; and there is John Sargent who sees the *Oyster Gatherers at Cancale*. There are those who see the broken glass, the open window, the scratch on the desk; and there is Sherlock Holmes who sees the scenario of a crime. The key to judgment is cohesion or synthesis—putting things together in a way that allows us to read what they mean. We all make judgments, and how we make them is an index of our character. It is in judging that we are who we are. How we read a passage, a gesture, a situation, or even the signs of a larger event reveals more about who we really are than any other act we do.

But we can also misread the signs or the passage. And when we do, we are ignorant, not in the sense of being denied information but of ignoring or overlooking the clues and keys that should indicate the proper coherence. It is not that an element is missing— that might excuse—but that the elements congeal into a distinctive whole that either distorts or reveals. Should we be held responsible for this? Perhaps it is the only thing that can invite responsibility.

But even if bad judgment be a kind of ignorance, why is it ghastly? What does this term mean? Its etymology is suggestive. "Ghastly" comes from "ghostly"; it is what we feel at the presence of death. To say he has a ghastly look is to say he looks like death. There is, in the ghostly, something terminal or final. We are uneasy because there is no further appeal or resource; it is ultimate. We are aghast at death because death is final and irreducible, hence beyond our power. To be aghast is also to be shocked, and for the same reason: we can do nothing about it. Yet, being aghast also implies what is unexpected; we are startled because we are beguiled by our expectations.

We are aghast at Othello's misjudgment—which is a kind of ignorance—not because he is unskilled at judgment but because he rightly is proud of his excellence in judgment. His ignorance is as dirt because, like dirt, it is base; that is, ignoble—not of the know-ing or noble class. But it is not the *effect* of his dirty ignorance that is ghastly, but that it is seated in his judgment. We should not—perhaps even cannot—make a moral decision concerning his ac-tion, for at the very least that distracts us. Rather we are asking what it means to be good and we see that, in part, to be good is to confront judging as supremely vital in being who we are. We are aghast at bad judgment because our capacity to make judgments is fundamentally *ours.* It is our judgment that mirrors our selves. To see a noble man like Othello make a bad judgment is like star-ing death in the face—it is ghastly—for both death and judgment are final and ultimately, our own.

In the history of philosophy there is a classical dispute about whether or not ignorance can be evil. Socrates seems to suggest that ignorance is the very basis of evil, a position thoroughly dis-credited by many subsequent thinkers, including Nietzsche who pokes huge fun at this Socratic suggestion by pressing it to its ex-treme absurdity: evil people then, are just *dumb!* But the Socratic view has its defenders, and one way to see it as a serious candidate is to locate the origin of true knowledge in judgment, so that igno-rance is seen as bad judgment. The sharp distinction between that metaphysically elusive power or faculty known as "the will" and the more epistemic power of making judgments thereby becomes blurred. This blurring serves the deeper metaphysical instinct for unity or synthesis, which may be a philosophical advantage. "Blurring" may be anathema to the advocates of clarity as the su-preme virtue, but undue multiplication of distinctions, especially metaphysically fundamental ones like "The Will" and "The Intel-lect" is inimical to coherence. The point is that, if we leave the metaphysics of capitalized nouns aside, we are judging beings, and to judge badly is not a mere epistemic error but a morally relevant action that can be censured. To confront such misjudging leaves us aghast, especially when the misjudgment is made by an other-wise noble person. Such misjudgment is ghastly because it de-nudes absolutely.

In ordinary cases where we ourselves are guilty of bad judgment, we are aghast at our own finite vulnerability. "How could I have been so *stupid?*" is not a plea for mitigation but a self-indictment of our own judgmental failure. This indictment reveals the esteem placed on judgment and the stunned disappointment that follows misjudgment. There is a certain status here that shows the importance of judgment, because most of us (unless we are remarkably arrogant) fully expect our allotment of shortcomings, faults, mistakes, and errors, which we endure simply as part of our humanity and that serve, if nothing else, to humble us in our pretensions. But although we accept these faults, we are not aghast by them. It is only when we are guilty (!) of bad judgment that we react in this stunned and negative way. We are not aghast when ignorance is excusatory—that is, when what is lacking is an item of information—but when our failure consists in putting together the pieces in a distortive way. To make a mistake does not disbar us from respectable company, but to misjudge forfeits our membership in the one company we honor most, namely, those who are acceptable to ourselves. It is this dreadful focus on our own reality as fundamentally lacking that so appalls us that we see ourselves as ghastly—as if we were facing death.

To confront our own ignorance as a source of being bad discloses the supreme importance of ourselves as judges. If the ghastly is deathlike, then the original judging must be lifelike. To judge is to be alive, to be who we are and not a mere clone of a species; it individualizes. Thus, in confronting ghastly ignorance we discover that who we are matters, and that an essential quality of this mattering is our capacity to gather things together into a synthetic whole. It is not necessary to reduce all evil to ignorance; we do not need to invent special metaphysical entities to account for it. We simply recognize that Emelia is aghast at the noble Moor's ignorance, and by the character of her reaction we discover there is a kind of ignorance that does indict. For, in essence, the ghastly is nothing else but the opposite of what judgment strives to achieve. To judge is to see the order in things; to be aghast is to confront the very disorder that bad judgment brings about. Emelia would be upset by Desdemona's death even if it had been by natural causes. What stirs her to ghastly outrage is the dirtlike ignorance that has so distorted and mangled what, when judged properly, should be beautiful and orderly. This ignorance does not excuse; indeed, it is debased because it is ignorance. It is ghastly.

Shameful Weakness

"Why did I not resist?"

It is the rebuke that most diminishes esteem; it is the censure that demotes utterly in spite of its wanton abundance. When our transgressions are accounted for by weakness, we are ashamed. "Could you not watch one hour with me?" he asked his friends; but they had fallen asleep, and he notes that though their spirits were willing, the flesh was weak. What is most curious about this phenomenon is that the bitterness of the indictment is most severe when wrought against ourselves. We are tolerant of human frailty in general, willing to overlook, forgive, excuse, or even embrace with avuncular fondness the less serious of the lapses, slips, and comic shortcomings of the species. But when we ourselves are exposed as lacking, there is an almost unendurable burden that presses down on our very existence and hence seems unshunable, like death. This is shame. If we truly are, as Nietzsche suggests, the beast with the red cheeks, it is of fundamental importance to isolate what it means to be weak and what it means to have that finger of weakness point out our shame. What does shame reveal?

This shameful weakness is not the mere limitation inherent in our finitude. We are not ashamed of our inability to feed the starving millions or cure the countless wretches of their agonies, for these are simply beyond our power. Nor are we ashamed of our own ordinary follies and dalliances we know we should avoid but do not. Shame follows only that weakness that threatens our own self-respect. It comes when the burden or threat is not greater than ourselves, but less than ourselves, so that in succumbing to its influence we are diminished. To be defeated by the mighty is no embarrassment, but to be defeated by the banal shrinks the range of our own reality. And this is the point that must emerge: It is not that we are first too weak and then, because of this weakness, we are led to failure; rather, it is in the failure itself that we *become* weak. It should be obvious upon reflection that, were my weakness an inherited or genetic flaw, there could be no blame in my subsequent misdeed. Weakness, in other words, is not the cause of shameful conduct; rather, shame itself is the weakening or diminishing factor.

Else were this a most brief remark: Those who are too weak to act properly will not do so, and shame is nothing other than the consequent feeling of inadequacy that follows improperly from misplaced assessment of one's capability. We no more expect the weak to act honorably than for the blind to appreciate a sunset or a cripple to dunk a basketball. But this causal account of weakness entirely misses the point.

The term itself is important. We call weak what *should* be strong, not what *is* not strong. The weak are not the frail. Weakness results from lack of exercise and proper diet, particularly, in the metaphor, the former. If my legs are weak because I have not exercised, then my failure to climb the ladder to save the child is not excusatory but shameful. To allow a great nation's military to grow weak by underfunding or bad administration does not excuse, but shames, the government. It is for this excellent reason that Aristotle points out that, by definition, the practical virtues need practice. One who never had to endure any privation or challenge cannot be expected manfully to endure great hardship. A diet of excuses does not feed, but starves, a child's character. To come up short in a challenge of virtue is therefore to indict not the single act of weakness but the entire history that leads up to it. And thus the indictment of shame berates not a particular act but an entire life of indolence or avoiding one's moral exercising.

Yet this Aristotelian account, though enormously helpful, still lacks satisfaction. What is at stake here is not a set of prescriptions that tells us how to act but an examination of the dynamics of our very soul in terms of the most elusive of all spiritual concepts: cowardice and courage. For if weakness indicts, it is cowardice; and if strength triumphs, it is courage. And by the very appeal to these terms the entire nature of the inquiry takes on a new dimension. There is a dilemma in seeking to grasp the essence of courage. On the one hand, courage seems to be equated with the simple agency by which responsible actions are possible. To do what one ought is to have courage; to be unable or unwilling to do what one ought is to lack courage—it is to be cowardly. The difficulty here is that the virtue itself either disappears entirely into the broader notion of agency or it becomes entirely mysterious. On the other hand, courage may seem a mere natural talent like bravery, possessed by some and failing in others, which makes it difficult to

appreciate as a moral notion. Yet, courage is obviously recogniz-
able in an almost universal way. Few do not realize that courage is
an admirable virtue that can easily be recognized. But what *is* it?

Even Plato, in the courage-dialogue, *Laches*, is reluctant to define such an elusive, though fundamental, term. But he does point
out the inherent dilemma in confronting the problem of fear as an
essential ingredient in being courageous—a fear based on ignorance, so that the paradox is inescapable: the greater the fear and
ignorance, the greater the courage. This is troubling since knowledge and not ignorance should appear the ground of the virtues.
The method of our present inquiry is not unlike that in the Socratic
dialogue. It is not to offer a digested and perfect definition of the
terms but to uncover the truth surrounding how we confront the
problem itself.

By directing our focus not on the noble and lofty concept of courage itself but on the weakness and shame that is its opposite,
some enlightened purchase on the problem may be uncovered. We
have noted that weakness is not a cause of failure, but that in
failing we become weak, and the weakness shames us. The shame
is thus the manifestation of being a failure *as* being weak. This is
important because we are thereby relieved of having to reify weakness as some sort of spiritual entity residing in the soul, like an
ulcer in a stomach causing discomfort. By unpacking the phenomenon of shame we note that shame diminishes us. It leaves us
flawed, so that we seek to hide or shrink away lest the flaw be
seen. It is not the flaw that causes shame, but it is being ashamed
that is the flaw. In being shameful we shrink, seeking in smallness
or shadows some hiding place. It is, as was noted in the analysis of
outrage, an impotence and a nakedness. The shameful do not wish
to be seen.

With these few hints, it is possible therefore to reverse the procedure. Being courageous means—and not courage as some kind
of entity or even characteristic of the soul that some possess and
others lack—being unashamed; that is, not hiding but revealing,
not diminishing but fulfilling, not covering one's nakedness but
glorifying what is hidden. Courage is, therefore—as an opposite of
weakness—the strength that is developed by the exercise of spir-
ited conflict, as the hard exercise of muscles builds the strength in
the body. Here the Socratic dilemma becomes a revelation. Cour-

age is not the absence of fear but the confrontation of it; it is not something other than fear *with which* we confront it but fear itself, faced. Indeed, fear itself is not some alien other "thing" that we face but the facing or confronting of the fearsome itself. Not to confront is to hide; it is to dissemble by turning away from our own ability to confront; it is cowardice.

The dynamics of this facing and not-facing provide a wealth of resources for the admirers of the human condition. In Stephen Crane's *The Red Badge of Courage,* the young soldier must first face his own shame in order to confront himself. He must first fear, and indeed fear greatly, before the fear can be faced. His courage is not on the first battlefield but in his panicky retreat, where he learns to accept his own fear. Or, in another context, Tennessee Williams's great drama about courage, *Night of the Iguana,* shows us that those like the Reverend T. Lawrence Shannon and the lacerated Miss Jelkes, both of whom fight dreadful battles—often losing—with their own private demons, are perhaps truly courageous in facing their own shame and weakness. Shame is thus not a mere consequence of a prior wretchedness, weakness; rather, shame is itself a wretchedness in which we seek to turn away from our own truth. Yet, paradoxically, shame itself can be redemptive by being confronted. To face one's shameful past is to be courageous. On the other hand, to be shameless is not redemptive, for the shameless do not confront themselves at all.

Neither courage nor weakness is a cause; nor are they qualities that some possess and others lack. We are rightly ashamed of our weakness, not as a cause of doing what is wrong but as a wretchedness, a mode of being that turns away from confrontation. Fear is a phenomenon that, when confronted we are courageous, when unfaced we are wretchedly weak and ashamed. By probing into our own shame, therefore, the truth of our curious strength in weakness is revealed. Strength, in this spiritual sense, must always be a strength in our own weakness, a confrontation of our fearing. To unface this fearing is to seek false solace in shame.

There is, after all, no little self-indulgence in unfaced shame. It is a perverse selfishness, as if fascinated by our own smallness and naked ugliness. Shame, when left unfaced, becomes self-pity, which is also a kind of insolent arrogance. On the social or political level it is the impotent and petulant anger at being "oppressed" or "victimized" by the powerful. But to seek solace in being oppressed is simply wretchedness in the extreme. Shame confronted, however, is redemptive. And so the curious paradox that so disturbed Socrates persists: it seems that only the fearful, in facing or confronting his fear, can be courageous.

What does this tell us about our guiding question, What does it mean to be good? To be good is to be courageous, but to be courageous is to confront our own weakness and hence our own shame. To be good thus is revealed as to confront our own being bad. But weakness is real, and the shame we feel in its presence is entirely legitimate. What this means with regards to being good needs to be considered after the final ground is sketched.

Abhorrent Character

"What have I let myself become?"

Some people are so proud they will bring down an entire country to redeem the slightest slight against their honor. Some are so malleable they will adjust to the noble as well as the base with untroubled ease, providing nothing on which to rely or depend. Some are so loving and kind they will sacrifice their very lives to help another. Some are so rapacious that no pleasure can be denied them, even at the cost of crime and outrage. Most are relative in their passions, perhaps spongelike in their variance, but with a few spines or ligaments that stiffen resolve in one way or another. They can be siblings, even twins, and differ so remarkably in character we cannot help but wonder how to think about it.

There seems to be something irreducible, even absolute, about character. David Hume, in his attempt to show us the fundamental difference between impressions and ideas, points out that we cannot imagine a gentle, kindly character ever understanding what it is like to be cruel. Does this mean that we are "given" our characters and, hence, determined by them? Or is Hume's insight only partially correct: Although a gentle character may never understand cruelty because he has no direct experience (or "impression") of it, perhaps he can, with the help of external, psychological trauma, change his character and learn to hate and hence be cruel. Perhaps the truly wicked characters, such as Stalin, Hitler, Charles Manson, Jeffrey Dahmer, and other vermin can, through remarkable acts of will and the assistance of loving therapists, become penitent and kindly angels of mercy. However we consider such questions there is no doubt that character seems the fundamental seat of judgment, strength, responsibility, and guilt. It is the one term we seem to identify most closely with our own reality. My character is my Self and, for whatever reason, this character identifies me as who I am. Character seems the personification of the "principle of individuation," and as such it has a special status in this inquiry.

When character, however, is seen as the ground of wrongdoing, whether in another or in ourselves, the consequent response is abhorrence. Unlike the ghastly and shameful, abhorrence has both moral and aesthetic dimensions to it because it offends not only our moral sense but also our eyes and ears. We do not want to be in the presence of such wicked characters, not because we fear them or even hate them, but simply because their very nearness is offensive.

It is important to reiterate that this inquiry is not concerned with the metaphysical questions of responsibility, so that whether or not these unsavory characters are psychologically ill or genuinely wicked and hence deserving of punishment is, for the moment, shelved. The question is: What does it mean to abhor a character that seems inclined by nature to be bad? And because this is a rather atypical question, it is fitting that the examples we use are those outstandingly vile personages that blot the pages of history and the electronic chronicles of current information. There are few monsters of this sort, but our abhorrence of them is palpable and undeniable. In point of fact, there are countless people whose characters inspire abhorrence—indeed our own character may inspire self-abhorrence often enough—but these responses are usually mitigated, perhaps even muted, by other considerations. It is not methodologically unwise, therefore, to focus first on the startling and the rare exemplifications.

What does it mean to abhor bad character? In abhorrence we turn away from what is foul in part because there is nothing we can do about it. In both weakness and ignorance there seem to be some hope of redemption, or at least there is the sense of righting the wrong through punishment or vengeance. But when the source of wrongdoing is one's character, neither rehabilitation nor punishment seems enough. Furthermore, in cases where the offender is weak or ignorant, there is some sense that the perspective of the offender is at least intelligible and perhaps even sympathetic. We are all weak and ignorant, so these faults are common. But we do not all have the same character, and if it is fundamentally an evil one we disassociate from it utterly by turning away from it in disgust. Far more than weakness or ignorance, when the bad is found in character, it is the person we find unacceptable, not the act.

And it is this *persona* that makes abhorrence so revealing. For what it means to be a person is as dear and precious as any realization we can hope to find. We are constantly learning, wondering, probing, and admiring this mystery of our own reality as persons, so that when the person *as* person defiles, we reject it utterly. We turn our faces away from any possible confrontation with it. In the phenomenon of abhorrence we express absolute rejection; indeed, the rejection is more fundamental than censure, punishment, or vengeance. For when we censure or punish we want the offender to exist so that he may pay for his crime; but in abhorrence we intend the offender not to be at all. This is not to say we wish to execute him, for that is to punish; rather, it is as if we wish to erase all existential meaning, to deny not only his future and present, but his past.

There is a certain form of punishment that approximates this reaction, namely the classical notion of exile. To exile an offender is to dislocate, to deprive him of any proper place or belonging, as if the very presence offends. In abhorrence we banish the offender from our home and presence because the very existence of the offender is a contagion. The contagion threatens the very wholesomeness of what it means to be a person.

To shift the focus from the abhorrence we have toward truly wicked characters (such as Iago) to that we may have toward our own character is to open deeply troubling truths about who we are. Extreme cases of self-abhorrence may develop into so black a despair that not even suicide is an option since it entails an escape that seems unearned. It is a mark of his genius that Shakespeare wrote the finally confronted Iago simply as mute. But this extreme is so inky that it may offer no light at all, and so we direct our concern to the less than total instances of self-abhorrence, bearing in the back of our mind this complete self-loathing that is possible, and that even the incomplete instances threaten to become.

Self-abhorrence is peculiarly fascinating because the very essence of abhorrence is to exile the offender from the offended, which, when both are one and the same, provokes a most unusual wrenching of the spirit. In trying to turn away from ourselves we simply re-confront ourselves, and the loathing waxes with every turn. There is no more wretched state possible than self-disgust or self-abhorrence because we cannot distance our sensitivity from our own stench. Yet, in muted degrees, we all confront this ignominy. But why dwell on it? Precisely because, in its fascinating decadence, self-abhorrence may well reveal one of the truest paths of uncovering what it means to be good.

There can be no abhorrence without character because character is precisely what we abhor. If its essence is "to turn away from—" then nonabhorrent character prompts a turning-toward. If exile is the sanction against bad character, then welcome is the boon of good character. To be good is to be welcome.

And who are welcome? First and necessarily are those to whom we belong, like family and honored friends; and after that any whose presence brings hope or delight. To be welcome is thus to be received favorably or to have some claim upon acceptability. It is to belong. The abhorrent do not belong. To possess the kind of character that is welcome, that belongs, is to be good. It is one of the fundamental ways, though not the only one, in which we understand what being good means.

What we find abhorrent in those whose character makes us turn away is not simple wrongdoing but a perverseness or nonhuman distortion of the presence that is either welcome or exiled. By "perverse" and "nonhuman" I mean qualities that are opposed to what is akin or welcome—that is, alien, foreign, strange. A figure like Iago is more than just bad, he acts out of motives and in degrees of intensity that do not seem familiar, acceptable, or even human. So distorted are his perspectives that he is unwelcome, and so we turn away in disgust at what is so unlike ourselves that it does not belong.

Indeed it is this unwelcoming exile from the human home that lies at the basis of what is, in effect, a dismissive judgment. We seem to want to label as insane those who are abhorrent just because tagging them in this manner excludes them from the welcome of the human community. A cruel, senseless killer is judged insane, not because there is medical evidence of compulsion but because were he assessed sane he would *belong to us,* and hence in a fundamental sense *is* welcome, just as an errant family member, in spite of his malefactions, can always return home. But our disgust and repugnance at inhuman character forfeits all welcome, and hence must be judged as not belonging. Not to belong to the human race is to be insane. But such judgment is entirely too facile.

Self-disgust is likewise a form of self-exile, in which we close all the doors of welcome against ourselves. If the origin of this abhorrence is our character, then we cannot disassociate ourselves from it as we might weakness or ignorance. We ask: Is this the kind of person I am? The term "character" comes from the Greek cognate meaning "engraved" or "stamped," suggesting that the form impressed upon us by our character is not a mere attribute, and certainly not a fleeting mood or disposition, but is of our essence. Hence to reject character is not to censure a mere attribute, but the fundamental kind of person one is. If self-abhorrence is an exile of our own character, then, its indictment is inescapable. This, of course, is ultimately unendurable, for we cannot exile ourselves from ourselves, and so it must be embraced. To overcome self-disgust there requires either a deep form of self-deception in which we deny the truth about our character or, in a splendid act of welcome, literally absorb ourselves into ourselves by widening the dimensions of hearth and home. The difference between this self-deception and this widening welcome is critical, for the former denies the guilt and the latter forgives it. All forgiveness is a broadening of welcome; it is not a denial of wrong.

What matters in the analysis of these three ways of being bad are their differences. There are at least three different ways to be bad; and if to be good is to confront them there must be at least three different ways to be good. There is not only one, single way to be good. To judge well, to be courageous, and to develop good character are all quite distinct; to let our outrage against any one of the three ways move us to redress the wrong is also distinct. It is not obvious that there is only one way to confront any particular mode of being bad. For this reason it is necessary first to unpack these phenomena in order to establish as broad a range as possible for being good, lest in focusing on one confrontation a distorted or unbalanced picture emerge. Our normal understanding supports this because we consider fierce and violent courage on the battlefield to be good. Yet we also consider a warm and generous character as good; these are not only distinct but even opposing in their nature. The same person may be good in one sense but not good in another. If then this preliminary sketch is even vaguely correct, there seems to be, in spite of these vast differences, a common element in all of these accounts. To be good is apparently always to confront the threat, temptation, tendency, or even the reality, of being bad. Being good is therefore a victory, a triumph over a genuine possibility of evil or wrong. It is not, as I noted earlier, the mere negation of being bad but a conflict with it so that, in the absence of possible bad, there can be no good at all. It would seem, therefore, that he for whom the greatest evil is most possible alone can achieve the greatest good. And this is the deeper sense in which the so-called naive view of what it means to be good is fundamentally true. Such a view, however, seems to thwart the notion that there are naturally good people, charmingly radiant by instinct—a rather difficult idea to suppress.

This initial, cursory analysis of the threefold ways to confront what it means to be bad now establishes more clearly the nature of the present quest. We must seek to understand judgment, weakness, and character more profoundly. Yet fidelity to the nature of the inquiry demands that these probings into judgment, weakness, and character not be direct, as if we were able on such slender evidence to pronounce ex cathedra on these lofty truths. Rather, each of these origins of failure can be approached by singularly distinctive yet richly concrete phenomena, the unpacking of which may offer routes of thinking that, like various spokes of a wheel, lead to a common hub. For reasons that unfold in each section, the following phenomena will be studied: comedy, which reveals the difference between the silly and the foolish; temptation, which reveals weakness and strength; and corruption, which reveals character and the lack of it.

3

The Foolish and the Silly

When that exotic but riggish gremlin of mischief, Robin Goodfellow, responds to the antics of the Athenians in the forest, he expostulates: "What fools these mortals be!" It is a supreme moment. We, the audience—ourselves mortal and foolish—gladly affirm this truth and hence seem, however briefly, to be judging ourselves from a quasi-divine perspective. There is, doubtless, a touch of gentle contempt in Puck's remark, but there is warm humor and even affection in our abetting it. The dramatic distance becomes a revealing mirror that not only reflects but somehow illuminates and even magnifies the truth of our own finitude, which, without the fondness offered by Shakespearean genius, might otherwise be too cruel a lesson to learn.

But what does folly mean in this context? Since it is our own folly, and we ourselves laugh at it, it cannot simply be ignorance, and surely not wickedness, since these are not laughable. There are times when the foolish are not be laughed at at all but severely censured and even condemned. A foolish misjudgment in war or politics is not funny but horrible; a foolish surgeon is a disaster, and foolish stockbrokers can dissipate a fortune. There seems generally little reason to affirm the foolish, for being a fool is to be vulnerable to the basest indictment of contempt. Indeed, is it not a kind of cruelty to laugh at fools? No one enjoys being laughed at or being called a fool, so perhaps there is something unsavory and indecent in our mockery of Bottom the Weaver. Perhaps Puck is simply pernicious.

But as a comic audience we cannot accept this. Granted, foolishness may at times be dangerous or even criminal; the antics of the love-anointed exiles from Athens are not only funny, they are warmly embraced in their folly with universal affirmation. There is, therefore, as great a paradox in comedy as there is in tragedy—perhaps even a greater one—for the lofty solemnity of great tragedy seems to redeem it but the inherent levity, perhaps even triviality, in the comic renders it dismissable. But no one should dismiss the great truth of *A Midsummer Night's Dream.* And it is because we do not dismiss it that the paradox stymies our attempt to understand it. How can anything so trivial be so important? Or, to ask the same question in an entirely dissimilar way: What does it mean to applaud our own foolishness?

Foolishness is not mere ignorance but a special kind of misjudgment in which what is misjudged is ourselves. In and of itself, folly is not comic. Lear, who dreads his own folly, beats upon his own head and laments that he has let his "dear judgment out," but his is a tragic plea. To lose "dear judgment," especially when it is about ourselves, can, in certain cases, however, provoke the gentle, intimate, and redeeming laughter that is the essence of great comedy.

To be foolish is to judge unwisely. When this lack of judgment exposes a universal vulnerability in a nonthreatening way and offers a reflective glimpse of our bumptious and inelegant frailty, denuding our self-deception and uncovering our misplacement in the scheme of things, we find a curious attraction to our own limitation. We are made friends to our own beguilement. It is the truth that comforts; the laughter is a release from the bondage of deception, especially the deception of pomposity.

It is here that a most important distinction must be made. It is a subtle distinction, almost elusive but of great significance. There are no ready, clear-cut terms with which this distinction can be sharply drawn, but perhaps it can be approximated by distinguishing between the foolish and the silly. The present context understands these terms as subdivisions of folly in the broader sense as self-misjudgment; that is, being foolish in the broadest sense of judging ourselves unwisely can be divided into being foolish in the comic sense and being silly. Normally the term "silly" suggests impropriety in the realm of the trivial, as when we say a petty, bureaucratic policy is silly because it is ineffective and senseless. But the silly can also become hugely dangerous, as when an ideological bias so distorts our vision that we misjudge with dreadful consequence. Outraged pride, vainglory, pomposity, and blinding arrogance are all silly—that is, they stem from irrational and petty distortions of self-importance—but they can have hideous and dire results. Academicians are often silly, and so too are unchecked political movements irreverent of learned wisdom. The difference between the foolish and the silly thus requires serious reflection.

Bottom the Weaver, in *A Midsummer Night's Dream*, is foolish; Malvolio, in *Twelfth Night*, is silly. The latter, though checked by the guile of other fools, is potentially very dangerous indeed; the former, in his very impotence, is redeemable and likable. Both are comic characters, but Malvolio is laughed *at*, whereas Bottom is laughed *with*.

There is a difficulty in accepting the comic unfolding of *Twelfth Night*. Malvolio—whose very name burdens him unfairly, since it means "ill will"—is after all, rather badly treated. Maria and the two ridiculous knights, Sirs Toby and Andrew, have deceived him with the forged letter. He is unjustly thrown into a prison, mocked, misled, and meanly tricked. Furthermore, he is in love with Olivia, and lovers are supposed to be revered in comedy. Even Olivia herself at play's end admits he has been sorely abused. He deserves our sympathy and even perhaps our pity. And yet, unless the production is badly botched, we do not feel sorry for him at all. Or if we do briefly pity him, the sentiment is soon canceled. And this is disturbing. For by all the canons of decency and respect for the victimized he ought to win our sympathy. But there is something about him that forfeits our otherwise legitimate compassion. Why?

Contrast this miserable creature with Bottom in *A Midsummer Night's Dream*, a fool if ever there was one. Puck's magic potion makes him into an ass, quite literally. He, too, thinks highly of himself. When the players are gathered together to be assigned their roles by Peter Quince, Puck demands that he be given all the parts. His diction is absurd—hearing with his eyes and seeing with his ears!—and he hams up the performance of *Pyramus and*

Thisbe to the point of ridicule. Puck and Oberon make him the butt of their sport exactly as Maria and her fellow clowns make Malvolio the butt of theirs. So what is the difference? Malvolio is silly; Bottom foolish. How are we to understand this?

There is much that is good-intentioned in Bottom, even if he is rather full of himself. Though his concerns are ill-grounded, he really does care about frightening the ladies with the lion's roar; eager always to please, to explain, to justify—though his attempts are outrageous—he overcomes obstacles by his sheer love of life and a deep respect for others. Note how he strives for politeness even with Titania's fairies. The asshead fits him well, and even he is amused by what the trick seems to tell him about himself. But Malvolio's arrogance is of a more sinister ilk, for he esteems himself superior on the basis of his moral rectitude. Unlike Bottom, his comic misjudgments do not stem from a concern for others but from the bane of all upright and pretentious men: vanity. He disdains all others, seeking self-elevation at the price of denouncing all human weakness. And when he discovers he has been unjustly treated, he categorically refuses to forgive. It is Maria who spots the nature of his insolence—she calls him a puritan. None are more intransigent in their misanthropy than the abused moralists who judge themselves upright and the world decadent. In laughing *at* Malvolio we seem to think he deserves his abuse, not because of what he has done, for his behavior is stiffly proper, but because his arrogant contempt for all who enjoy life stems from his deep, puritanical unwillingness to accept frailty in others and certainly not in himself. In laughing *with* Bottom we rejoice not at his deserving his clumsy misadventures, but with his ridiculous yet generous acceptance of them without rancor. Bottom actually understands himself far better than Malvolio, for he is full of wonder; the puritan is full of hate.

Yet the distinction between the foolish and the silly is not merely that the former are good-hearted the latter malevolent. This appeal to Bottom and Malvolio is merely to initiate the terms by examples. Both the foolish and the silly offend reason, since both reflect bad judgment. But in addition, the silly offends our sense of self-acceptance. There can be something deeply puritanical in the silly that is lacking in the merely foolish. It eschews forgiveness precisely because it takes rectitude so very seriously that it becomes a fetish; but this is to distort rectitude into a self-serving power. Malvolio's love for Olivia is, at root, a love of power because he sees in it an opportunity to enforce stringent behavior under the guise of propriety but really as an indulgence of his own putative superiority. Not all silliness is puritanical, however. It can also be giddy and irreverent; but in either case it inspires a wanton lust for power that emasculates foolishness and is thus entirely retrograde to comedy itself. Nothing is more inimical to comedy than puritanical or irreverent silliness. The comic genius delights in fools but must outwit the silly. Thus the well-intentioned but hugely foolish Dogberry constabulary defeats the silliness of Don John's irreverent villainy in *Much Ado about Nothing;* and the puritanical silliness of Angelo in *Measure for Measure* is defeated by the comic forgiveness of the Duke. It is tempting to say that fools take the trivial seriously whereas the silly take the serious trivially—and the latter is very, very dangerous and the former is very, very innocent, and hence fun. Both are bad judgments, of course; but Erasmus praises folly not the silly.

It is essential for comedy to defeat Angelo and Malvolio, for these two puritans are a threat to the very essence of the comic art. It is not merely the historical fact that the Puritan parliaments of England wanted to, and eventually did, close down the theaters because of their frivolity. It is also because, even as characters within a comic play, the success of the silly guarantees a failure of the foolish. The silly giggle like geese at the victims of their own plotting, the foolish laugh at themselves, for the silly is always slightly shameful, the foolish always overt. In the silly we alienate ourselves from the warmth of universal mankind; in the foolish we embrace the finite with an acceptance of our faults.

Both the puritanical and the irreverent are hence paradigms of silliness. It may seem, however, that irreverence is necessary for any comedy and should rather be seen merely as foolish; but the truly foolish, like Bottom's crew and the Dogberry constabulary are not irreverent at all, for they revere the very things they make us laugh at. Bottom is profoundly in awe of both the importance of the play and the solemnity of the court; Dogberry reveres, if curiously, the law. To poke fun at the pomposity of institutions is not to be irreverent toward them. Quite to the contrary, when comic genius pops the balloons of self-importance, the consequence is not that respect for the noble is diminished but enhanced. Both Beatrice and Benedick disdain marriage, yet by the end of the play their own disdain seems a kind of reverence. Indeed, in most comedies love itself is grossly toyed, but Hymen's entrance at the final act shows how the folly of love is its greatest reverence.

It cannot escape notice that both irreverence and puritanism are excesses of what originates as noble sentiments. For surely concern for rectitude, which is the original sponsor for what deteriorates into puritanism, is a worthy passion. But puritanism takes this laudable urgency for doing what is right and distorts it into excess by bloating it out of proportion to our finitude. It is therefore a distortion or disharmony of what it means to dwell in the world, and is hence bad judgment. Irreverence, too, begins as a laudable endeavor, though it is the opposing vice to the puritanical. We seek originally to scoff at the pretentious and the self-important, both of which themselves are misjudgings. But this scoffing at the usurpatory trappings of the elegant deteriorates into a contempt for the elegant itself. In both the puritanical and the irreverent, then, there is a perverting or bloating of a good instinct into a silly one. The essence of both is distortion through bad judgment.

The irreverent is perhaps less obnoxious than the puritanical, for both in its foolish and its silly manifestations there can be laughter; yet this very fact makes it more sinister.

Falstaff is for the most part foolish, but when he begins to drift near the throne, his bawdy, irreverent antics take on a serious threat and so Prince Hal must reject him. There is a legitimate lump in the throats of the audience when this happens, but its endurance is essential for the triumph of Young Henry. It is foolish and hence forgivable to let the crown prince flirt with the unsavory and half-criminal underworld, since it does no lasting harm to the state. But it were silly indeed to let the fat knight into the corridors of power and judgment. The case of Falstaff is of profound importance in seeking to comprehend this subtle but critical distinction because it shows exactly how the silly differs from the foolish. We have warm feelings for Falstaff in *Henry IV, Part I* and even in the early parts of *Henry IV, Part II*; though there are moments when the true blackness of his irreverence warns us of the impending judgment, as when he grossly abuses the corpse of the noble if misguided Hotspur. But there simply cannot be anything but relief that Falstaff is halted from introducing comic misjudgment into the castle of his king—for that would be not only foolish on Henry's part but silly. The foolish is therefore comic only when limited to the ineffectual, else it becomes silliness and hence dangerous. To play with the profane is foolish; to play with the sacred is silly—for that is sacrilege. The deconstructionists are Falstaffian in this sense: As long as they play outside the castle of truth they are merely comic; to allow them to play with truth, as they do, is silly, and cannot be condoned. It would, in fact, be ghastly.

How do these reflections fit into the broader question of this inquiry? The present search is for a philosophical understanding of judgmental knowledge, the lack of which constitutes one of three essential ways of being bad. In seeking to pinpoint what it means to judge at all, we are now focusing on a specific kind of bad judgment called folly, which has been provisionally identified as a misplacing of one's proper position and importance in the world, due to improper assessment or fitting together of the things we confront. It is, in other words, a kind of incoherence. But in order to qualify as folly, it must be an incoherence or misplacement of ourselves. Within this self-misjudgment is a further distinction between the silly, which is self-incoherence that defies redemption or forgiveness, and the foolish, which denudes or reveals our finitude and hence is both redeemable and forgivable. The foolish takes the ridiculous seriously; the silly makes the serious ridiculous.

To be silly is to be bad, for the way we congeal or cohere the various elements of our informational knowledge into judgmental knowledge or self-deception is due to who we are. The censure in being silly is not that it results in unacceptable consequences but that it originates in our own self-understanding that has perverted or misread its own meaning. To learn about our frailty in this regard can itself be a kind of wisdom—what might be called comic wisdom. To fail to learn what this means is a silliness that destroys all capacity to judge and hence is ghastly. Good judgment—which now must paradoxically include the learning of our finitude in comic reflection—is essential for being good. What makes it good is not the acquisition of knowledge but the learning of truth.

This discovery is fundamental. I have already suggested that to be good is possible only and always in terms of the confrontation and struggle against being bad. To learn of one's folly in a way that allows us to embrace it—as in the rare kind of laughter found only in great comedy—is one of the basic ways in which this battle is constantly being carried out. As mortal we cannot ever avoid entirely our own folly, which is simply to say that, even with all the information needed to succeed, we can force the pieces together in an incoherent way and thus still fail. But when this failure itself becomes a resource for learning who we are—as we so learn in comedy—the discovery provides a special kind of self-coherence that is good judgment.

And so the question now is: How do we confront silliness? If to be good is to confront the bad, and if to be silly is to be foolish in a nonredeemable way, then we must confront this "bad" kind of foolishness. But the reflections on the comic plays shows us exactly how to do this: we confront—and hence overcome—the silly, not by the intensification of the dour, the grave, and the solemn, but by comic foolishness itself. Comic folly is the antidote to the bane of silliness. To laugh *with* Bottom is possible only if we see our own folly in him and hence laugh at our own finitude. To laugh *at* Malvolio is to disassociate ourselves from the very blindness of a silliness that cannot laugh at itself. When the silly giggle at themselves it is because they delight in their own cunning and elitist superiority; the fool laughs rather at the truth of our own finitude.

But these reflections, which are easily available to anyone who submits to the enchantment of Shakespeare, tell us a great deal about judgment. To be able to judge ourselves well is not an a priori faculty inherent in the privileged few, but is to let learning happen. And one of the most rewarding ways in which this self-learning can happen is to discover, through comic laughter, how to embrace our own foolishness without being silly. For supreme silliness is not to be able to learn. It is good to learn. It is above all good to learn about our own folly, which learning in turn directs and grounds our being able to judge.

To judge is to read what it means to be in the world. To be in the world can be misread. But both the good reading and the misreading themselves are essential to being in the world, and hence they contribute to our ever widening learning. It is not the simple mistakes we make in reading the world that makes us silly but the failure to learn from them. Bottom's awe at what he calls a dream compels him to seek out Peter Quince to write a poem about it; his own folly becomes a source of wonder and hence learning. Malvolio's discovery of the letter's forgery does not produce awe or learning but simply hatred, self-pity, and an intensification of his sad silliness. To be able to judge, therefore, presupposes our already being in the world. One cannot judge from outside the world. Indeed to be deceived into believing one can judge from outside the world is to be silly. But if to be good is to confront what it means to be bad, and being bad as being silly or even foolish is to judge as already in the world, then to be good is likewise to be in the world. So we cannot be good outside the world; that is, goodness is not other-worldliness. The silly, though they are in the world, refuse to recognize this and hence deceive themselves. The foolish celebrate their being in the world and hence can laugh at and learn from their misreadings of it.

To be good is to be in the world. It is therefore a certain kind of theological silliness to plant the saintly or the goodly in celestial emptiness because this places "The Good" (written now in capitals) beyond us. Or, what may be worse, it places the puritan and the irreverent outside the world, unredeemed by laughter, and capable of judging others *as* others, that is, as bad. From this perch the judge cannot be judged and self-learning cannot be possible. This is supreme silliness. Of course, once The Good is placed outside us, beyond our reach, there can be no shame in being bad and so all self-judgment ceases. For self-judgment to be eclipsed by such silliness is absolutely bad, not only because what it means to be good is now no longer thinkable but because all learning is also forfeit.

These reflections on the silly and the foolish have uncovered a tremendous truth about being bad and being good; namely, that the struggle is a part of our *belonging* to the world.

To belong to the world is not only to be in it but to be able to be good in being in it. It is ours. It is our home. To become alien to our own origin is thus a kind of misjudgment as to who we are. It is a kind of foolishness that, if not embraced as a denuding lesson, can become silly and hence misplace us entirely. To insist that being both good and bad must take place within the world wherein we belong may well be the most important philosophical discovery thus far in seeking to understand what it means to be good.

4

Temptation

What does it mean to be tempted?

The phenomenon of temptation is of extraordinary philosophical importance, yet it is rarely addressed by inquirers into ethical or moral reasoning. We are all tempted, we have all yielded, and we have all, at times, resisted; and we know perfectly well the anguish and relief of these experiences. Perhaps because temptation seems such a denuding phenomenon, exposing as it does our frailty and venality, we seem to disregard it as a theme for inquiry, preferring the more abstract and nobler issues of morality and justice. Yet, in order for there even to be such a thing as temptation, being good or bad must first matter; that is, to be able to be good or bad is a fundamental presupposition for temptation to occur. And so it seems that reflection on temptation must await the prior and loftier enterprises of determining just what it is we ought to do and what allure there is in evil that would keep us from doing it. But the method of this inquiry begins with the concrete phenomenon of temptation because this is something we confront directly. And even in its direct confrontation there is already this remarkable discovery that what it means to be good or bad must now matter. We know it must matter because unless it does there would be no genuine temptation, and we are genuinely tempted. Temptation is thus the concretization of good and bad mattering; it is this concrete phenomenon and not the abstract formulation of principles that must concern us first.

But the phenomenon must be genuine. It is entirely meaningful to read about Mephistopheles tempting the gifted Faust, but it would be ludicrous for him to tempt Sir John Falstaff. We must, in other words, focus on temptation as an authentic conflict between the lure to yield and the reluctance to submit. If either the lure or the reluctance is pale, the learning will be minimal or nugatory. A thirsty man is not tempted to drink a glass of cold water because there is nothing to impede him; one sated with postprandial contentment is not tempted to begin a second meal, for there is no allure to provoke the appetite. To understand temptation is to realize that both reluctance and allure are present. For the sake of inquiry, indeed, it is always better to study instances of temptation in which both are of sufficient persuasion as to agonize the tempted even to the point of anguish. It is only because Don José is a loyal and devout soldier that the temptation to abandon his duties by the gypsy girl Carmen compels our attention and Bizet's genius. Carmen had seduced many others before Don José, and warned him she would seduce many others after him, but his reluctance to yield and her allure to persuade him to yield are of such intensity that when the martial cadence of his regiment clashes Wagner-like with the motif of her seduction, the music achieves a power of dramatic illumination, showing us what it means to be torn apart by such conflict. Were José indifferent to, or even casual about, his military oath, there would be no tragic truth . . . and no counterpoint.

The lure of evil is no more fascinating than the courage of reluctance to yield to it, though our popular literature would convince us otherwise. There is guile in the persuasion that evil is somehow more entertaining than the drab, almost banal, intransigence of the steadfast. But great literature reverses the ranking. Three examples of temptations found in such writings will be dissected to expose the ligatures of reluctance in spasmic torment with the sinews of allure.

In Thomas Mann's *Death in Venice*, the famed and gifted author, Gustave von Aschenbach, having discovered in the city of canals a beauty that threatens his control and decency, realizes he must abandon the allure of Venice and so decides he must check out of the hotel. But a small snag of chance intercedes; his baggage is sent awry. Using this as an excuse, the artist hurries back to the Lido, his heart aching with a "reckless joy." In leaving the city he was doing what was noble and right; in returning he was submitting to a dread contagion of spiritual defeat. Why did he leave? Why did he return?

It is not bad for von Aschenbach to love Tadzio, nor is it bad to want to be near what is beautiful. The artist's return to the city is not a prelude to some seamy and passionate seduction of an innocent, for that is not in this artist's character. It is, of course, bad that von Aschenbach keeps Tadzio's family uninformed of the pestilence, hazarding his beloved merely to allow him more opportunity simply to gaze upon the radiant youth. But what really matters, what explains even this inexcusable jeopardizing of the Polish family to the plague by his reticence, is his own self-corruption. His reason for leaving Venice, therefore, is to avoid this corruption in his soul.

Mann's literary skill helps to reveal the profound syndrome of what it means to be tempted. Early in the story, von Aschenbach sees an older man, disgustingly barbered and cosmetized to disguise his maturity, playing with youths; a spectacle that arouses in the artist a feeling of vile repulsion. At the end of the story, however, the great man allows his own barber to dandify him as well— to make himself attractive to the boy. The disgust he felt at the old dandy is now turned upon himself. How did he become so corrupt?

It begins, as most temptations must, with artful self-deception; artful because, though deceptive, it is based on truth. Von Aschenbach, upon his first fascination with the boy's radiance, accounts for his thrall to it in terms of an artist's love of pure beauty. It is an aesthetic, almost philosophical regard for ideal perfection, the way an artist is entranced with a flawless embodiment of form, not the way an appetite is stirred merely for gratification. But although these are the terms Mann uses to depict what Aschenbach feels, he also manages, with a cunning so subtle it deserves the sobriquet "genius," to inform the reader that, though these artistic sensitivities are undoubtedly there, so too are the erotic ones. And it is here that we note the first stage of all true temptation: the guile by which we use legitimate language to masquerade the truth, which is too harsh to be accepted directly. And the deception continues.

Aschenbach accounts for his growing unease by appeals to the meteorological contagion of the city, whereas we recognize the contagion of his spirit. But these deceits are as yet insufficient, and the troubled artist decides, regretfully though nobly, to escape the pestilence, both figurative and literal. He plans to escape the city, as well as his own self-destruction.

The trunk is falsely delivered. Aschenbach leaps upon this opportunity as if it were a godsend, though he knows it is sent from quite the polar resource. He greets this turn of fate with a "reckless joy." Why? Because what is fated is beyond our hegemony. Since we do not control it, we are not responsible for it. One wonders if the trunk had not been sent awry whether Aschenbach would have found some other trivial excuse to derail his journey. For subsequent to self-deceit, it is the derailing that always interrupts the trek of the steadfast. We seek, in our being tempted, distraction. For only in distraction is the reluctance reluctant. Although we call it an excuse, its proper name is distraction, the way an enemy battalion feints to distract the commander from the brigade's attack. Once Aschenbach, already weakened by his deceitful language, is distracted from his exodus, he submits entirely to the vagaries of fortune. Or, to speak in truth, he submits to the slavery of his passion.

We all do this, of course. We know that when honor or duty clashes with desire, desire outmaneuvers honor first by deceptive labels and then by distraction from our own commitment. All we ever need do is cease concentrating, and we will gladly yield. The reckless joy or gladness inevitably follows this submission, for it is what we desired all along. Honor, as the enemy to desire, is outflanked by distraction.

What Aschenbach desires, therefore, is not to control but to be controlled. And what better pair of deceptive terms to wreak this alien mastery than fate and beauty? Are these not worthy adversaries of our out-generaled army of control? Beauty deserves its homage, fate admits of no resistance. Nothing emasculates as an appeal to what is inevitable, or even common. "Everybody does it" derails integrity just because we take joy in our shared species, not because we emulate the masses. "It's just human nature," is another echo of the same deceit. For Aschenbach, the twin appeal to beauty and fate may seem of nobler origin, but it is of the same stock. Whatever guise we want to give it, it amounts to surrendering our control to forces greater than we call our own.

Before his attempted exodus, Aschenbach, as artist, worshipped beauty; now he submits to it. Even the reader is reluctant to censure too harshly, for after all, is not the reverence for beauty what makes an artist? And this is the third discovery, after self-deception and distraction: we are not tempted to *do,* but to *be,* or rather, to *become,* since we become other than who we are. Aschenbach is not tempted to do anything, but to become the opposite of his nature. For Beauty does not tempt us to pleasure, but to bondage. His character is well provided by the literary genius of Mann—his work habits are rigorous, his style "chiseled," his habits regular, his decorum conservative. He is a man of control. His stern duty alerts him to the danger in Venice, and he takes the proper steps: he plans his departure. The temptation is not to return to the fetid city, for that is a mere means—it is rather to become estranged from his own nature, to submit recklessly and joyously to powers he does not command, fate and beauty. The former, is, of course, an excuse; there is nothing fateful about the misdirection of his baggage unless he wills it, or allows it, to be a distraction. But the bondage of beauty, for one who had mastered it for so long, becomes a metanoia, a complete reversal of one's entire persona. No longer the grim overseer, he becomes now the elated slave. And this is one of the deepest insights inherent in all temptation: the secret desire to be controlled, to surrender the terrible burden of freedom and responsibility, to yield up our own person to be absorbed in the greater wash of the abstract, the dictatorship of the species. Yet, even in this grim capitulation, Aschenbach cannot entirely exile his native judgment, his artist's eye. For as he now basely crawls through the pestilent streets of the sickened city, he cannot disbar his own comic contempt, the artist's last refuge. He laughs pathetically at his own ruin, the exchequer of character now so impecunious he has no purchase to extricate himself, for he discovers that he has not marketed his soul to the wealth of beauty, but to the pathos of its mastery. Ever since that moment in the train station when he learns of his wayward trunk, he knows that what tempts him is not the taking of an action, but the acceptance of an alien role. He becomes other than who he is. We are not tempted to act, but to be.

That I can become other than I am through submission to abstractions, unworthy of their control over me, is a shameful yet
joyous deception. It is not primarily what we do that shames us,
but who we become. For our ignoble actions flow from an ignoble
character, a character we have adopted in the lure of temptation.
Thus, it is not the bad action that makes a bad man, but a now-
weak man whose surrendered strength mocks his slavery, that
does a bad action.

This sketch of the fall of Aschenbach cannot replace the richness
of Mann's inspired depiction, but we can use it to focus on the
three stages of submission: first, deceit; second, distraction; and
third, abandonment of who we are. By this reflection we learn that
what we call "weakness" is not some excusatory lack that causes
misdeeds, the way an ulcer in the stomach causes pain. Rather it
is a self-deceived, self-generated distraction that derails us from
the track of who we are to the siding of an impotent and unimpor-
tant train of artificial delight.

Perhaps the grandest deceit of all is the whimpering protest of
irreversibility. It is not that we cannot resurrect our original selves,
it is quite simply that we will not. The slave loves his slavery, else
he would not be a slave. The three stages of temptation are not
mere precedent conditions that then vanish; they are continuing.
The trio of self-deception, self-distraction, and self-eclipse is entirely misnamed when we call it "weakness"—for to call it that is
simply self-pity, a stage of corruption into which Aschenbach does
not fall. But this trio of temptation's syndrome does provide a response to the second howl of the wrong-doer's distress: "Why did I
not resist?" It is a gruesome and denuding question. No less so is
its response.

But why should we resist at all? Perhaps by far the most enlightened step we can take is amused contempt at these struggles
against our nature. To speak of temptation is quaint, perhaps even
naive. As Sir Henry Wotton, in Oscar Wilde's novella *The Picture of
Dorian Gray* so famously puts it: "The only way to get rid of a temptation is to yield to it." This is but one of the many delicious *bon
mots* that sparkle with ominous but delightful frequency throughout the story, which is written almost entirely in dialogue, giving it
the flavor of a drama. Wotton's brilliant and sophisticated dis-

missals of morality and propriety are often ascribed to Wilde himself; but any serious reading of this profound work reveals that the author is not unequivocal in support of Sir Henry's contempt for nineteenth-century Christian ethics. Indeed, Sir Henry provides us with an excellent model of the tempter. In this Faust-like tale, Wotton is a glib and charming Mephistopheles. Having probed into the inner workings of the darkly tempted Aschenbach, it may now be of considerable value to examine temptation from the perspective of tempter.

The story is told on two levels: as a fantasy and as realistic study of a tempter's skill. The handsome youth Dorian has his portrait painted by his artist friend, Basil, who succeeds in capturing on canvas the boy's beauty and innocence. Under the gifted persuasion of their mutual friend, Sir Henry, Dorian is convinced that the painted beauty on the canvas is to be preferred to his own fleeting youth, and he expresses his willingness to surrender his very soul if the roles of flesh and canvas could be switched, so that he, Dorian, would forever remain radiant, but the painting would grow old, wrinkled, and ugly. Through some unspecified mechanism of the preternatural, this actually occurs, and as the years pass the painting ages and decays, whereas the actual person himself continues to look forever a mere eighteen years old. The fuliginous consequences of this fantasy constitutes the fascinating plot-structure in which Dorian Gray is transmogrified from a decent and moral young man into a morally corrupt and sinful wrecker of lives, until finally he meets a deserving if wretched end. This is the first and fantastic level.

On the second level, however, is the far more serious story of the tempter, Sir Henry, and the tempted, Dorian Gray.

Sir Henry Wotton's temptation of the youthful gentleman is almost diabolical in its cunning. In a manner so gentled with sophistication that all seriousness seems excised, Wotton cleverly weds his disdain for middle-class values with his praise of Dorian's natural but fleeting beauty. He makes it seem as if to be young and beautiful requires that one be indifferent to propriety and principles. Most of Sir Henry's friends can laugh at these suggestions, and indeed the reader is never completely assured that Wotton himself believes them. But the vulnerable boy believes them utterly. Dorian falls in love with an actress, Sibyl Vane, who, in response to a cruelty of Dorian's, takes her own life. It is Wotton who convinces the boy not to regret this, but to live life to the fullest, contemplating the suffering of others from an amused distance. And it is this distance that allows the otherwise upright lad to deteriorate into a monster. At the beginning of his deceptive life, Dorian attracts those who, because of his icy but lovely presence, destroy themselves, leaving Dorian convinced that he is not responsible for their torment; but eventually after many years he is driven to murder his friend Basil who had painted the portrait. Inured by the indifference of sophisticated disdain, not even this dreadful act upsets his decorum or placidity. He lives a charmed life, escaping detection of his crimes by seeming miracles of fortuity, and all the while his painting, now hidden away in an attic, grows more and more hideous. Only Sir Henry seems his constant and untroubled friend.

Sir Henry Wotton's temptation of Dorian Gray is almost a paradigm. He tempts by an appeal to excellence and good taste, almost as if not to yield were itself a crime against one's own superiority. It is not a temptation based on the desirability of this or that consequence, but a contempt for all reluctance to yield whatsoever. Yet, it is not merely a generic temptation to do bad things in general, but a very specific allure to become a very specific kind of person: a superior being who, by his charm and purloined youth deserves to be excused from normal moral restraint. Charm is a kind of self-indulgent power, and power, far more than pleasure, distracts us from our truth. In such temptation we matter more than what makes us matter, a clever, cunning beguilement of such intricate dissembling that few can resist it, since it does not even seem like resistance.

The mocking of the portrait, with its manifest corruption is a brilliant device. For Dorian is thereby sequestered from the consequences of his own depravity, which serves first to enhance his sense of invulnerable power and license, and then finally to fill him with loathing, until at last he strikes out at his own image with tragic results. It may seem that the magic of the painting bearing the original's guilt has nothing to do with Wotton's temptation by sophistication, but a moment's reflection reveals that providing a distance from one's own guilt—which is what the picture does—is exactly what Sir Henry's inky *bon mots* achieve. For part of their attraction is the realization that with this self-adulatory dismissal of common virtue there is a deliberate deception of self with image: the artist becomes the art-work, and vice versa, and that is utter wickedness.

Aesthetic distance is absolutely essential for the truth of the art-work to occur; but when this distance is applied to our own moral reality, the consequence is not truth but evil. For Sir Henry's allure really amounts to treating moral judgments as aesthetic judgments, and that is profound dissembling. It may be the most deceitful of all lures, for it misprizes the very worth of beauty into a distortion and corruption of truth. For all his cleverness, Wotton is a cheat, and his victim is his friend, the gullible youth Dorian Gray. Dorian also cheats, by way of the transfer of his real guilt to canvas; but this transfer victimizes himself. It is the triumph of semblance over reality, and that is the essence of wickedness.

The three stages of temptation discovered in the analysis of Aschenbach—self-deceit, self-distraction, and self-eclipse—are all here as well, but they are so artfully disguised as sophisticated charm that they deceive even as they reveal. Wilde's story is actually an indictment of art as a way of life rather than a way of truth. That the author himself may well have been guilty of precisely that confusion is both sad and remarkable. For the picture may not be what it seems: It is not Sir Henry who reflects Wilde, but Dorian Gray.

This is, of course, not a moral lesson telling us how to avoid temptation, but a philosophical one in which truth is the only goal. Yet, even this distinction, though entirely valid, gives us pause; such distinctions are never absolute nor as rigid as they may seem. It is, after all, the aesthete's seduction rigidly to distinguish the good from the beautiful, as Sir Henry does, and thereby corrupt the integrity of thinking. We must distinguish the moral from the aesthetic, but not to the extent that we set them over and against each other. Thus a central theme in Wotton's temptation of Dorian to *become* an aesthete is the disintegration of our thinking into nonrelated compartments, totally self-sufficient, like Leibniz's monads. To tempt well is thus akin to the warrior's craft: divide and conquer. To learn of this is to discover something of massive importance for being good: integrity, in the literal sense—being whole and complete. To be good is to integrate all the modes of our

reality into a harmonious unit, accepting our duties and pleasures, our shortcomings and our triumphs, as a mosaic of interlocking tiles that together constitute a single base. To be *able* to be
tempted is to affirm both the uniqueness of each tile as well as
their interdependence; but to *submit* to temptation is to fracture
the adhesion of this union. In the aesthete's case it is to disjoin the
beautiful from the good so severely that the latter seems an insult
to the former; it is to separate the living canvas from the living
model, and to watch in contempt as the one grows old and the
other grows unseemly. It may seem odd that *to be able* to be
tempted provides the integrating cohesion, and *yielding* to temptation provides its dissolution, but the study of Wotton and Gray
shows us why this is so. We are, in essence, temptable; hence to be
good is not to be void of all temptation—that is mere innocence—
but to confront temptation with the cohesion and coherence of integrity. It is not by accident that it is the *picture* of Dorian Gray
that reflects the truth, whereas Dorian himself is but a poser.

The biblical account of the temptations of Christ, together with
Dostoyevsky's reflections on this in *The Brothers Karamazov* provide the final example. In Matthew 4, Christ, after fasting forty
days and nights, is tempted to change the stones to bread, but he
rejects this by saying we do not live by bread alone. This may seem
a simple appeal to Christ's hunger after a long fast, but Dostoyevsky has Ivan point out a deeper lure. Were Christ to perform a
miracle of this sort would make following him a necessity; for who
would not follow someone who could turn stones to bread? When
probed, this reflection is of terrible, even awesome, significance.
Christ is being tempted to succeed. He is lured into performing an
act that would guarantee success of his mission, for miracle work-
ers attract, and providers of bread attract, but one who provides
bread by miracle simply cannot be resisted. It is the very theme of
this section of Dostoyevsky's novel, called *The Grand Inquisitor,*
that God would save mankind only if we be willing; that is, only if
we save ourselves. The power of salvation comes from God, the
willingness to accept that power comes from us. When, after the
third temptation, Satan asks Christ to worship him, he in effect is
asking Christ to assert his authority, to save us by power. For who
else is Satan except the embodiment of celestial power, whose

struggle against God is against the withdrawal of power, the way parents slowly and achingly withdraw their authority over their children to let the children become adults. But this is the risk of Being. The great struggle between good and evil, which is anthropomorphized symbolically in the accounts of the war between God and Satan, is the ultimate reality; it is the struggle between power that rules and power that lets be. It is the struggle between guaranteed salvation and free, and hence risky, possibilities of being saved and failing to be saved. Hence the greatest temptation of all is not to do what is wrong, but to become unable to do what is wrong. For it is only the capacity to do wrong that makes doing right meaningful, and hence even possible. To be tempted, in other words, is to confront our own being able to be good or bad; so that to submit to the greatest temptation would be to make temptation impossible. But only the truly evil or the completely innocent are incapable of being tempted. Being tempted makes being good *possible*.

There is nothing original in the claim that the struggle between being good and being bad is the fundamental metaphysical reality. Empedocles argues that four elements are guided by the principles of love and strife. Kant argues that the only legitimate metaphysics is a metaphysics of morals. Schopenhauer accounts for reality by an appeal to the blind forces of the World Will in conflict with the independence of mind. Martin Luther King argues that all reality is fundamentally moral reality. John Milton's lurid accounts of the great battles between the Archangels Michael and Lucifer make the struggle between good and evil the origin of all that happens. Whether mythological or philosophical, these accounts manifest a sensitivity to fundamental thinking: The struggle between being good and bad is original reality. The concretization of this struggle is temptation.

"Why was I not able to resist?" This plea for understanding, though legitimate, is also dangerous. For if the answer is: "Because I am weak," the peril lies in thinking of weakness as a cause, which then weakens all the more. For there is a "second order temptation" that excuses and hence trivializes the wrongdoing, by blaming it on some unknown flaw.

Weakness is not the cause but the effect. We note the three-fold scenario of temptation: self-deceit, self-distraction, and self-eclipse—and a part of self-deceit is that weakness is an excusatory cause. We find, in the reflection on Dorian Gray, that an essential mode of both self-distraction and self-eclipse is the fragmenting of our wholeness, artificially dividing beauty from its consequences. But an appeal to "being weak" as a cause of failure is also a kind of fragmenting of integrity. And finally, in the brief visit with Matthew and Dostoyevsky, we see that the greatest temptation of all is to yield to the lure of success based on the power to enforce rather than on the power of letting-be.

If the failure to resist yielding to a temptation is due to an inherent weakness, we abjure all temptation whatsoever: we are like the thirsty man "tempted" to drink cold water—the term loses its impact. But if, on yielding to a temptation, we howl with the question "Why did we not resist?" and mean by this to provoke a tormented search for the original wholeness or integrity of what has been ruptured, then the question confronts rather than avoids the struggle. The implications of this for the guiding question of the whole inquiry—what does it mean to be good?—are enormous. For at the very least we see that to be good is to be tempted. To be able to be good or to be bad is meaningful. Even submission to the lure, which results in our *becoming* bad, is not meaningless: the fallen are not without hope. Only those who dismiss temptation entirely forfeit the possibility of the cohesive integrity that is fragmented by doing wrong. What it means to be good, therefore, cannot be successfully probed by probing only into success.

5

Corruption

There seem to be three distinct, though often overlapping, sources that account for the kind of person we are. The first stamps us from the onset with certain inherited traits that identify us as belonging to a specific type. Some of us are born aggressive; others shy and retiring; some are self-oriented, others warm and generous by nature; some loud, some quiet. It is difficult to deny that many of these qualities are simply inherent in our particular make-up. Although now discredited by science, the earlier doctrine concerning the five humors, generating the sanguine, melancholic, bilious, phlegmatic and choleric personalities, was actually a fairly useful taxonomy for identifying basic types; and were this view presented merely as a classificatory model for common psychology, and not as physiologically grounded in a causal way to actual fluids in the system, such distinctions may well have persisted in our nontechnical usage. It is a pity to discard such a convenient and harmless system of labels. But whatever language we have—and I am not sure that "type A" personalities really succeeds as well as "sanguine"—we do seem to accept the belief that certain personality traits are genetic or inherited; and that these traits contribute, though not exhaustively, to what makes us the kind of person we are.

The second source, often contrasted with the first by the disjunction between "nature" and "nurture," is that which molds us, particularly in our youth and childhood, into members of a social order. We know of undisciplined children put into various institutions of severity, such as schools, religious programs, or the military, and emerge after a time of apprenticeship, into influenced models of decorum. We seem to believe, in other words that moral training is indeed possible, just as the Jesuits of the Enlightenment said it was, although perhaps not quite to the extent promised. Certainly in a less rigid sense, most of us agree that early familial influence can form or shape a personality to considerable extent. Quarrels doubtless arise as to which of the various institutions, familial, economic, religious, or educational, is the most successful; and further quarrels develop over which of these resources, nature or nurture, is dominant. Like all unanswerable disputes, these become rather boring, generating heat rather than light; but few are willing to deny that both play some role in making us who we are.

But there is a third source. It is fostered from within, as when we consciously adopt habits, attitudes, and ways of thinking, in order to develop according to what we judge we ought to become. For the sake of terminological precision, I consider the first two sources to influence or account for our *personality;* the third alone I reserve for *character.* This does not deny that the elements of personality have some influence on our character; obviously they do. But the extent to which character has any moral significance, it must be isolated, as least formally, from the psychological resources provided by nurture and nature. For just as we seem to accept the influence of genetic inheritance and the environment on the development of our personalities, so too we also seem to accept the role of our own influence on our character. This is to say that we determine our own character, at least to some extent; and *to* this extent, we guide our own becoming. When we ask in stunned abhorrence, "What have I become?" we therefore are not seeking excusatory refuge in genetic or environmental factors that shape our personality. Rather we indict our own preceding story that has led us to this censure of our character. An essential part of this "becoming" may well be due to our allowing the environmental and genetic factors or our personality to deviate from the path of our proper role, or even to distract us from our integrity.

It is bad to let this happen; and it is good to develop our character in a virtuous way. Indeed, as will be shown, virtues are nothing
else but the several ways in which we develop good character. So a
doctrine of virtues is impossible without character.

The denuding question "What have I become?," when faced with
our own being bad, thus censures the moral development that allows us to become bad. We can call this development corruption.
Thus, in addition to bad judgment and yielding to temptation there
is the third way of being bad: becoming corrupt. This third way,
however, is the most wretched, for it suggests a pervasiveness and
persistence that the other two lack. To become corrupt is to undergo a change in our very existence; it is not only to *be* wretched,
it is to *deserve* to be wretched. To extricate ourselves from this
state requires a painstaking re-schooling, or perhaps even an un-
learning of the educational disaster that we let happen in our own
descent. These education metaphors are not random. For to become corrupt is to learn how to be bad. Corruption is not merely
submitting to a series of temptations that, after time, becomes a
habit; for that is mere spiritual fatigue. Rather, in corruption we
allow our character to be darkened so that temptation in the strict
sense is simply impossible. In the previous chapter it was noted
that a sine qua non of temptation is resistance to the allure; but
for the corrupt there is no resistance, hence no temptation. Indeed, corruption is exactly the opposite of temptation, for the former actually embraces its own deterioration. It therefore deserves
the designation "bad learning"; in corruption we *learn* to *become*
bad. Fundamentally, all learning allows us to achieve our own becoming. As we absorb our language and culture, assimilate our
values and discover and develop our talents we *become* a member
of this community, a master of this art, a defender of these beliefs.
Thus to learn is to become who we are, as an English child learns
to become English through learning how to be English-speaking,
sharing the history, identifying with the culture, and so forth. To
learn therefore is not primarily to gain knowledge but to become a
certain kind of person. When we take this syndrome and apply it to
corruption, we see that it is possible for us literally to learn to become bad. How does this happen? The first stage is the development of an achieved indifference. To justify our acts we assume
the false judgment that such acts are not really wrong; and this is

done either by (1) resisting the impulse to make a moral judgment at all, (2) discarding the principles that measure it as wrong, or (3) appealing to factors or overriding concerns that allow for putative justifications for what is normally censured.

Each of these three ways of achieving indifference is familiar. In the first case, having offended someone, we simply do not let ourselves think about it—we put our moral machinery in neutral, so to speak. This is a form of self-distraction, except, unlike that involved in temptation, it occurs after the act, not before. In the second case, we dismiss the entire moral apparatus as legitimate, pretending to doubt the efficacy of morality in order to avoid its censure. "Who's to say what I did is wrong?" "I should not be held to middle-class morality." In the third case we assert privilege. "Yes, terrorism is morally wrong, but it's necessary to support the revolution." Regardless of which of these three tactics is used, the effect is to numb the moral sense by assuming indifference or contempt to our moral restraint. Most of us have slipped into these modes on occasion, but are able to resurrect some sense of shame or regret so as to resist becoming entirely altered. If this indifference, however, achieved through these various tactics, is not countered by even a delayed contrition of sorts, we learn to grow entirely amoral, nodding only occasionally to the precepts of good conduct merely for prudential reasons. It is their very ease and convenience that makes these tactics so ominous.

This achieved indifference is but the first stage in the learning that leads to corruption. For the adoption of an attitude of indifference in and of itself need not corrupt. The second stage, as is the case in all learning, is reflective. Only after I learn to speak English can I reflect on its beauty and become vulnerable to its poetry; only after I have mastered elementary geometry can I step back and wonder at its elegance and exactitude. Similarly, once unfettered from the shackles of morality, I then can take a perverse delight in my own libertine indulgence. I can, in other words, reflect with approval on my own moral neutrality, dismissing with scorn and amused contempt the bovine meekness of morality itself. I become a transmoral aristocrat, delighted with the new license of yielding to whatever whim or bauble distracts me. This is essentially a reinforcement by reflection, which is always a fundamental second step in any educational development. It reinforces because we can, under the influence of the reflection, locate ourselves in a hierarchy in which we seem superior. The adages of Sir Henry Wotton and the acceptance of them by Dorian Gray are self-congratulatory and disdainful in this way. It is vanity. But the third stage occurs when this libertine self-indulgence finds itself so unpracticed in moral matters that we become prey to any lure that imprisons our judgment. We become slaves to a passion, or even to a distraction, because, beguiled by a false sense of freedom, we have no resistance to any enslavement that promises new titillation, gratification, or arrogance. We enter a heady bondage of refined gratification, no longer controlling our character but submitting to the terrorism that blinds. We become corrupt.

When we have knocked down all the barriers of restraint, and stand gleefully unfenced in the new open field, the realization that the carnivorous predators of the forest, our basest perversions, are now free to take us over entirely, we are forced to ask: What have I let myself become? It is the nadir of this educational descent; for we have become students or learners of our own depravity and vulnerability. In this empty meadow bereft of all moral fences, the wolves of disgrace may take us off as bleating victims—and we ourselves have torn down the walls. To become our own malignancy, to infest our own soundness with the cancer of complete license, is corruption. Under this influence, the sweet and gentle sweetly and gently poison children; the brilliant brilliantly enslave a whole generation; the privileged, privileged to torment the innocent; the strong, strongly profane the sacred. All of our own talents, skills, and qualities turn against our character. Like Dorian Gray looking at his own portrait in disgust and abhorrence, we see that corruption has made us repugnant to ourselves. We have graduated from the college of self-abasement; and we know with apodictic certainty: this is bad.

And so the threefold educational descent of becoming corrupt consists first of achieved indifference, then of amused self-reflection, and finally of total submission. What does this tell us about what it means to be good? It is the educational slant that is so revealing. If it is bad to learn self corruption, it must, correspondingly, be good to learn to achieve noble character. This learning to achieve noble character is found in the practice of excellence called virtue. And it is the study of this learning that is so profound. For the virtues are not what is learned—rather, the virtues are the *learning* itself.

The virtue of courage is to learn to confront fear; to learn to confront unanswered wrong is justice; to learn to confront our ignorance is wisdom, to learn to confront the infinite is piety, to learn to confront ourselves is nobility. These may not sound like the traditional accounts of virtue, but the reasoning is not only consistent with the analyses of what it means to be bad, it also has its origins in some of the greatest speculations in the history of thought. For in Aristotle's *Nichomachean Ethics* we discover that the practical virtues must be practiced. But what is achieved through such discipline is not the virtues themselves, as if courage, justice, piety, and wisdom were the goals, though Aristotle himself seems to speak this way. Rather, the virtues are the educational *means* by which we achieve nobility of character. To be sure, this is not Aristotelian orthodoxy. But just as surely it is a profound discovery in the quest for understanding what it means to be good, and the origins of the argumentation do lie in the wisdom of Aristotle. The metaphysical foundation of this discovery is that we are not static entities, rather we *become* who we are. The epistemology that follows is that *learning,* and not *knowing, is* primary: we learn to become who we are. The path of corruption is to learn badly; that is, it is to become fragmented and out of control through various vices, particularly self-deception and moral indifference. The path of virtue is learning, understood in the sense that the virtues are themselves ways of learning, not what is learned. To become, as thinkers, is to learn who we are, and to learn is to become who we are. Thus, learning cannot be reduced to the mere acquisition of knowledge, for in learning we become other than what we were. Corruption distorts this learning, so that we learn to become alien to ourselves, even other than ourselves. The fact that we can become corrupt reveals that in true learning we become noble, that is, not alien but welcome to ourselves. This learning is the practice of virtue, which means that the virtues are ways of learning to be welcome to ourselves, i.e., noble.

But this is to expand prematurely beyond the limits of the method. Reviewing briefly, we see that we indict our own being bad in three ways, censuring our ignorance, our weakness, and our character. In response to the first, we analyzed bad judgment, distinguishing the silly from the foolish. In response to the second, we discussed the meaning of temptation; and in response to the third we unpacked the phenomenon of corruption. We learned from these three negative approaches that to be good is to judge well, have strength or courage, and learn and become who we are by practicing virtues. These are surely not unexpected discoveries; indeed, they seem almost simple. But rooted as these discoveries are in the phenomena of bad judgment, temptation, and corruption, they now afford a concrete base from which a deeper interrogation can spring. Yet, the inquiry is still preliminary. The negative approach, seeking to understand what it means to be good by first unpacking the concrete phenomena of being bad, is not complete. Though the three central ways of being bad have now been considered, there are two consequences of being bad that now must be probed before we can proceed from indirect to direct inquiry.

6

Punishment and Forgiveness

A thief takes from his victim a hundred dollars. Upon capture, he is required to pay his victim fifty dollars. Even a child knows this is insufficient. And so, on further deliberation, the captive thief is now required to return the original sum in its entirety. But what does this mean? Again, even a child might realize that, though the victim now has his property restored, the thief has not suffered in any way for committing the crime. Why not steal if capture merely means returning what was taken? The possibility of escape always remains, and failure to escape offers no dismay. Perhaps, in addition to returning the money, the thief should pay something for the assault against the law. That is, the thief should suffer. To some thinkers, that we suffer at all seems a defect in the entire moral and metaphysical order. God's nonexistence is inferred from this putative defect, apparently because to be able to suffer at all is seen as inconsistent with goodness and the power to bring it about. Yet, if the previous paragraph is coherent, unless we were able to suffer, there could be no justice. For justice in its most primitive and original form means that the wicked are punished, the good rewarded. If this fundamental response does not occur, then neither moral judgments nor good conduct matter—they are but idle fantasies of a naive romanticism. Therefore, to be able to suffer is a necessary condition for justice. Nor is this principle valid only for the punishment of others. Plato points out in the *Republic* that a virtuous man who commits a crime seeks his own punishment, for as virtuous he desires justice in himself first of all. He cannot *be* just unless he be punished, so he actually desires to be punished. Having done a wrong, and given the option of selecting between a place where suffering was possible and where suffering was impossible, we would be forced, by this reasoning, to select the former. By dint of this reflection, it is impossible to judge that all suffering is bad. Indeed it shows that, at least in the case of punishment, suffering is good.

To punish is thus to inflict suffering in order to let justice matter. And yet, as simple and straightforward as this argument may be, it is hugely disturbing and at the same time richly rewarding. We do not say that because there is authority (such as the state or parent) therefore there is punishment; rather we say because there must be punishment it follows there must be authority— that is, some institution to inflict and determine the enforced suffering. What it means to punish and be punished is therefore prior to and presupposed by any institutionalization of justice. It is necessary to understand punishment in order to understand what it means to be just, which constitutes in part, though not completely, what it means to be good. Reflection on the thief being punished shows that the imposed suffering is not meted out for the sake of deterrence. Even if no one else were to steal ever again, the repayment by the thief merely of the amount stolen does not satisfy, for the offense is not merely against the victim, but against justice itself, or its embodiment, the law. We do not punish criminals as a warning for others, but to answer an offense. This becomes especially clear when Plato's virtuous man demands his own punishment in order to just; such an offender need not be deterred at all. Yet he still seeks punishment, the way the unclean seek cleansing. But this seems to suggest that the punished submit to some principle or reality higher than mere need to restrict behavior to acceptable limits or to rehabilitate the criminal. It is as if, having violated a law or having performed a bad act, the offender owes some endurance of suffering to be offered up to someone or something. That is, the phenomenon of punishment is, in its essence, neither deterrence nor rehabilitation, but an exercise of fulfillment or repayment, intrinsically worthwhile, and necessary for our being good. To be able to be good is to be able to endure punishment.

But how is it possible for our suffering to become an offering? In what way is the endurance of pain metaphorically similar to the unwashed being cleansed? And to whom or to what is this offering made? It may be rewarding to initiate this inquiry with a variation of this last question. Can we punish ourselves? Our preliminary reaction to this question may be so obvious an affirmative that sufficient probing of it may sadly be forfeit. Hester Prynne, in *The Scarlet Letter* is punished by the church and city of Boston to wear the red letter "A" on her bosom, but her fellow adulterer, Arthur Dimsdale, is forced to endure his punishment privately. He flagellates himself, torments himself, tortures himself, inflicting pain upon himself even greater perhaps than that inflicted on Hester. Surely, therefore, it would seem that Arthur, nobly and legitimately, punishes himself. Or, should we perhaps rather say he is the agent of the church's punishment? He is punished, not by himself but by the church, though it is through Arthur himself that the punishment is inflicted. Why might we as lief say he is the agent of another's punishment, either God's or the church's, rather than to say he punishes himself? If Arthur literally punishes himself then his suffering if offered to himself, and that is either perverse or profane. Punishment always presupposes the greater reality, the higher rank, the nobler prosecutor. The criminal not only, or even primarily, offends his victim; he offends the law; and the law is greater than he, just as the community outranks the single citizen. If sin be an offense against God, then to be punished for it is to endure suffering as a bestowal of oneself to the divine. And so the state, or the law, or the church, or the parental institution of the family, or God himself, punishes—and the suffering we endure is offered to the dominating reality as payment for the offense. If Arthur merely punishes himself, he becomes the recipient of his own offering. This, however, is incoherent. And so, to be precise, we say rather that Arthur, as a deputy of his church, punishes Arthur, the sinner. It is thus the church who punishes. We do not consider the hangman or the jailer as the punisher; they are merely carrying out, as agents, the will of the true prosecutor, the state. So Arthur Dimsdale, like the jailer, is a deputy fulfilling the will of the true prosecutor or punisher, God, or perhaps the Boston church. With this analysis, then, it seems we cannot punish ourselves.

Even so it seems a rather subtle point. Why is it so important to locate and identify the one who punishes? It is important because of what it reveals about being punished. To be punished is to yield something precious through the endurance of pain on behalf of an achieved obligation; it is to *suffer rightly*. Once we recognize that it is not the victim who has the authority to punish, indeed it is not the authority of any *person* at all, but only of an institution or divinity or office, the very meaning of punishment changes. Rightful suffering—an odd enough concept just in itself—can be inflicted only by authority, and the submission to that authority reveals that our own becoming occurs within a belonging. It is because I belong to this community that I can even break a law at all; and it is only as a member that I can be punished. It is the communal authority—i.e., the law—that punishes. There are two presuppositions that must be met, therefore, before *punishment* is possible. I must *belong*, and I must be able to suffer meaningfully. To be able to suffer as a bestowal on behalf of my belonging is to make possible my own becoming good. Thus, only possible sufferers capable of belonging can be good.

To be bad is to deserve punishment. This means that to be bad is to be able to suffer rightly, which is to say, to be able to endure inflicted suffering as an answering response to an achieved indebtedness. To be able to be bad is a necessary presupposition for being good, so that only possible sufferers are good. But the "achieved indebtedness," necessary for punishment, can only be found among those who belong; it is part of what "belonging" means. So only those who belong can be good. It is impossible to make sense of suffering induced by punishment if the sole factors in our calculus of propriety are the right of individuals and the principle of happiness. Punishment becomes a euphemism for deterrence, rehabilitation, or even protection of society from violent people. To punish in the sense of inflicting suffering as an answer for achieved indebtedness is simply repugnant to the utilitarian thinker. For such thinkers, to punish in the literal sense is merely to yield to the darker and unworthy instincts of vengeance and revenge. Yet, to incarcerate someone merely to deter others from doing the same act that led to the indictment is to use someone for the sake of someone else. To punish someone for doing wrong is to respect them for their moral importance. To focus on the problem of punishment solely from the perspective of individual rights is to deny that we belong, and that as belonging our cohesion as a people is sacred. The sanctity of this belonging together, being violated, is reinaugurated only if it is possible to suffer rightly. Punishment is thus not some dark, medieval remnant grudgingly accepted for pragmatic reasons, but an essential and fundamental factor in our understanding of what it means to be good and to be bad. Indeed, to be able to punish and be punished is philosophically more fundamental than the achievement of decent behavior and even than the execution of justice itself.

Up to this point the focus has been guided by the question, what does it mean to *be* punished? It is now needful to shift the question, and ask what it means to punish. If no person, merely as individual, can punish either himself or another, to be able to punish consists in belonging to a punishing institution, from family, to community, to nation. To suffer rightly on behalf of our own belonging is consistent with both our integrity and nobility; but merely to endure pain or harm imposed by another equal to us is nothing other than to extend the quarrel initiated by the original wrong. Therefore, what it means to punish is to extend nobility to those who share a common belonging, insofar as this nobility consists, in part, of letting justice matter. And it is this belonging to a shared nobility—the only kind of nobility possible—that allows for an *offered* suffering. To offer is to submit what is dear to, and for the sake of, what is precious. That this offering, in the case of punishment, may be enforced and violent does not detract from its being offered. To punish is thus to enforce the importance of belonging by allowing for rightful suffering. Justice, which means to be good insofar as we belong, is concretized in punishment. The difference between the negative concepts of revenge or vengeance, and the positive notion of punishment, therefore, is simply that the former lack this element of belonging that allows for rightful suffering. Only a private person or persons can wreak revenge; they cannot punish. Only institutions of belonging can punish; they cannot wreak vengeance. To belong to a punishing institution, therefore, makes rightful suffering possible.

But not every wrong is answered in punishment. Perhaps in

some rigid, puritanical logic, every wrong should be punished. But it is possible to forgive, even though forgiveness is always technically a violation of justice. Forgiveness is the concretization of this following truth: that belonging is what makes justice possible, and not the other way around. For if justice made belonging possible, forgiveness would always be an offense. Every act of forgiveness therefore concretizes the extent to which our belonging has greater range than being just. Yet, the fact that forgiveness must violate the formal and precise understanding of justice requires that this notion be subjected to a most strenuous scrutiny. For something as dear as justice can be sacrificed only by the most extraordinary of appeals. Forgiveness cannot be sooted over with loose or imprecise usurpations. Unfortunately the term is often abused and the notion itself distorted by license. What commonly is assumed to be forgiveness is far too often something quite other. Some rubbish needs to be cleared away at the onset. To excuse, to mitigate, to bargain, to justify on grounds of higher purpose, or simply to fail to censure by inattention or distraction are all distinct from, but often confused with, forgiveness. To forgive is possible only under the following five conditions:

1. The wrong-doer is guilty and deserves punishment.
2. There is no moral claim that can require forgiveness to be granted.
3. The forgiven is granted pardon solely on the basis of his belonging, and is ranked as worthy on the grounds of who he is, not because of what he has done.
4. The pardoner, in forgiving, sacrificially accepts the dread burden of the unanswered justice that is thwarted by the pardon.
5. The pardoner forgives solely as the vicar or the agent of an institution or power capable of graciousness.

These rather stern requirements restrict all pardon to gracious bestowals to one deserving punishment on behalf of an esteem anchored in the worth of belonging.

Whom do we pardon? A parent pardons a child simply because the child belongs to the family. Therefore, when a parent fails to punish a child because the child may be overly traumatized, or as a special bargain for some future conduct (We won't punish you this time if you promise to try harder . . .), or simply because the punishment "won't do any good," such leniency *is not* forgiveness. Only if the parent consciously and overtly recognizes the legitimacy of the punishment but forbears to enforce it because the child is beloved, and because the child is *their* child, is there true forgiveness. The injustice inherent in all forgiveness is not dismissed as if it were irrelevant—for how can justice be irrelevant?—but is absorbed by the pardoner. He takes upon himself that burden. The pardoner then must either himself endure the payment that would reestablish justice; or endure the burden of having thwarted justice. Were this fourth listed criterion not included, justice itself would simply be disregarded, and forgiveness would be bad, not good. To be able to forgive is possible only because what it means to be good has greater range than to be just; but unless justice is somehow honored by this outflanking known as forgiveness, the conflict would be misological.

When two friends quarrel, and one apologizes and the other accepts, there is no true forgiveness—though we may call it that in ordinary talk—because there would be no punishment. When the elder son pushes his younger sister off the stoop, the father, as the deputy of the familial authority, should punish his son. But were he to forgive him because of paternal love, the younger daughter's outrage must somehow be answered or at least absorbed. Merely to disregard the youthful gestes of the son, without the solemn instruction that and why he is forgiven, along with some compensation to the offended daughter, were merely to abet a licentious contempt for both children. We forgive because we love or revere the shared belonging of the miscreant, which is why we forgive our children, our family, our compatriots, friends, and those bound to us by love or law. To punish them when punishment is needed is not to love them less; indeed at times the educational value inherent in the punishment may show an even greater love. What, then, determines when punishment should be inflicted and when forgiveness should be granted? The question is unanswerable. For if forgiveness *should* be granted, it is not bestowed, and hence not truly forgiven. Furthermore, to codify a decision procedure by an appeal to a rational principle completely forfeits the nature of forgiveness, which must always be granted and never required. The forgiven are pardoned because of the worth of "who they are"—this is my son, so I forgive him—and is punished because of what they do. Therefore, to be forgiven is not to *be* good, but to *receive* a good. Can we, however, say that it is good to forgive? The puritan must say no; but in dismissing his answer we cannot dismiss his reasons. To forgive is good only because to forgive entails sacrifice. And what we sacrifice is very dear indeed. It is not only justice, but the sureness and security of being just, that we hazard when we forgive. The burden of censure shifts form the offender to the forgiver, for unanswered wrongs must have a target. Merely to say: "Because I love the offender, I forgive him" is not enough; for that sponsors wanton romantic license. Such is not really forgiveness but simply indifference, or worse, a self-indulgence that preens its own largesse. We cannot forgive from our abundance, but only from our sacrifice. And thus, true forgiveness is good, and being good, reveals that the range of justice is not as ample as that of goodness.

In the opening paragraphs on the discussion of punishment it was shown that in at least one case—that of enduring legitimate punishment—suffering is good. We now discover another way in which suffering is good: to sacrifice. But this opens an entirely new venue, the extent to which what it means to be good is not limited to justice or perhaps even morality. Before turning directly to these troubling but fertile questions, however, it may be beneficial to consider an entirely separate problem that can serve as a transition from the negative and indirect concerns to the positive and direct reflections on what it means to be good.

7

Can the Good Do What Is Bad?
(Transition)

It is sometimes difficult to believe what is written about him in the history books. Not only because of what he himself does, but what he somehow inspires others to do. Do barefoot, half-naked men gaunt with fatigue and hunger, all under his command, really cross ice-crusted rivers with waters up to their chests, and yet cheer him when he passes on his magnificent gray? Do they lay down their lives gladly for him, though he be stern and demanding? Perhaps it is because we now live in a less sacrificial age, or a less honorable one; or perhaps it is simply because we have grown so jaded with the empty promise of war we simply prefer not to consider or believe in the warrior virtues. Yet the historians who tell us about him are not romantic dreamers; they are, in fact, both cynical and detached. So we accept these remarkable anecdotes of his leadership and almost stunning valor but do not fully comprehend them. Those he led have left a legacy of personal reminiscences that are simply too numbered to be discredited; but those he defeated, those who were his enemies, are no less reverent toward him. Though they strove mightily to crush him, they still admired him. He is even now honored by his enemy. Yet, he was a killer of the young and a traitor to his government. His undoubted genius was not harnessed to advance science or art, music or poetry, or even statecraft or business. Rather his brilliance, courage, leadership, and cunning were directed at carnage and death. He defended a social and political order that supported one of the most heinous and contemptible institutions the modern world has experienced. On his magnificent steed, Traveler, he guided hungry warriors to bleed and shed the blood of others for rebellion; his mastery was in the service of human bondage. Yet they who fought for as well as against him judged him noble and honorable. They even judged him a gentleman.

Not all did, of course; nor do all presently. But those who howled and shrieked for his head in 1865 are not well favored by history. And his present detractors, dismissing everything about him because of a pacifistic rejection of all war, seem somehow no less strident than his contemporary haters. But we cannot let the assessment of those who chronicle our history disarm us from our own judgment. For there is a terrible problem that plagues our thinking about Robert Edward Lee: he seems a noble, perhaps even a good, man; yet he did a bad thing. If, in supporting the Confederacy he was perpetuating the indentured servitude of an entire race, believing as he did that slavery was wrong, how can we attribute to him all these lofty virtues? How can a good man do a bad thing? To ask this is not to ask if an ordinarily good man can suffer a lapse or stumble—that is not the question. We do not judge Robert E. Lee to have stumbled—except, perhaps, at Gettysburg.

Indeed, this is not even a tribunal before which we judge Lee. Rather, we look at Lee as a paradigm of the philosophical question: Can we *be* good even as we *do* what is bad? And to make sure that the intensity of the question is not vaporized by indirection, we precise the question even further: Can we, as good, do what is bad? Perhaps, of course, the matter is much simpler: perhaps Lee was not good at all, but simply bad. Knowing of his character, prismed through the flattery of the ages, to assess Lee as a bad man may actually be a more astonishing and difficult enterprise than to say he was good but did bad things. For then we must say that his bad action forfeits entirely all the virtues that his ragged, starving soldiers attributed to him. Either way, the judgment is terrible. We may, of course, escape the onus of it by pleading ignorance or an unwillingness to judge another, especially one enshrined in such distant, if glorious, memory. But though such reluctance is defensible, in the present context it is a distraction. We are not divine agents prosecuting before the tribunal of eternity the strengths and failures of one man as if we were counsels in a court. Lee presents a problem. There is much about his character that shines forth as enviable and worthy of respect. Indeed, he seems to belong to a very small number of historical figures who seem to deserve such admiration. There is nothing stinting, petty, mean, small-minded or self-indulgent about Lee. He simply did something we consider to be highly dubious—he defended the Confederate nation, which sponsored slavery. He himself hated slavery; he himself resisted the secession by his beloved Virginia; and so he was not beguiled. We cannot excuse him on the basis of ignorance. Nor do we measure his undoubted affection for his homeland as an excusatory passion that eclipses the anguish. For we do not seek to judge Lee, but to confront his story so that we can learn a truth: Can the good, *as* good, do bad things? So it is not Lee himself, but the question that haunts us when we consider this magnificent though anguished man. In this, we refuse to be distracted by the genuine possibility that Lee judged his allegiance to Virginia to be paramount, making his fell and dread decision morally defensible since he acted out of his perceived sense of duty. For that is to determine our judgment on the basis of something we cannot know. The question is not whether Lee acted in accordance with his perceived duty; rather it is whether anyone, Lee included, can be good, and *as* good, do what is bad. The historical Lee, presented to us by the scholarship of history offers us a fascinating embodiment of that action, and so we focus on him to show what it means to confront such a problem. False assessment of his true character merely results in the misjudgment of a man; we are primarily interested in the problem.

It can therefore legitimately and safely be assumed—though certainly not known; but assumption suffices—that Lee is a good man who, being good because of his many attested virtues, acted in such a way as to deserve the legitimate censure that what he did was bad. The possibilities of misjudgment in no way distract from the terrible question with which this assumption has left us. For if our assumptions are possible and coherent—not necessarily accurate—then we are faced with a vexing dilemma. In a serious way, in a nontrivialized way, Lee, properly cleped as good because of his manifest virtues, committed an act, willfully and knowingly, that he ought not to have done. He has, in other words, nobly done what was ignoble. Unless we are troubled by this, the present inquiry has no teeth. To be able to be good and do what is bad were impossible unless what it means to be good is not exhaustively determined by our actions. Once we permit of a fundamental difference between being and doing, the logical possibility of the good doing what is bad is established. For it then becomes at least formally coherent. Yet, even to permit of such a thing as a possibility, to say nothing of it ever being actual, is entirely disturbing, for it seems to open a floodgate of dangerous license, skirting all restrictions to behavior on the basis of an unmeasured subtlety grounded only in verbal eristic. It is not intended by this suggestion to emasculate the absolute authority of the moral law, nor to deny that what we do matters greatly in determining whether we be good or bad. On the contrary, the raising of this question is designed to uncover the profound integration between doing and being good. But distinctions that refine our understanding must precede all unifying synthesis that provides coherence. Philosophical precision demands that if a distinction is possible, even if it be dangerous, it should be pressed, else the naive assumption of unity is grounded in deception.

To speak of virtues is to speak of character; to speak of right or wrong actions is to speak of the moral law that determines what ought or ought not to be done. Even in ordinary, everyday language we speak differently of these two distinct, yet obviously interrelated, phenomena. Character is never static; we are always becoming, learning, changing, and growing. The virtues are the ways of learning good character; they are not what is learned, but the learning itself, as courage is the learning to confront fear. The moral law, on the other hand, is absolute and universal; it is not changing or becoming. To learn to confront unanswered wrongs is the virtue of justice; to submit to the universal truth that one ought to keep promises is to be moral. It may be a psychological fact that unless I learn to confront unanswered wrongs by means of the virtue of justice and learn to confront my fear in courage, I will be unable to do what I ought to do by keeping a difficult promise, but such psychological connection neither conflates the distinction nor accounts sufficiently for the interconnection. The language of the virtues and their opposing vices that mold our developing character is entirely distinct from the language of morality that determines what we ought or ought not do. If a good character can do a bad thing, it is possible only because of this important difference in how we think about virtue and morality. This difference in thinking is reflected in the contrast between two major philosophical traditions: those who approach goodness from the study of the virtues, such as the ancient Greeks and their contemporary defenders; and those who, like the Christian advocates of the divine law (sometimes called Natural Law) or who, like Kant, derive the Categorical Imperative from the nature of reason itself, approach goodness from the notion of morality. For the latter the question is primarily one of adherence to laws and principles, focusing on duty or obedience to reveal what one *ought to do.* For the former, the emphasis is placed on the development of good character and living a life of excellence or virtue. The analyses of these views must be delayed until the subsequent section; they are mentioned here solely to provide a reference or basis for making clear the present question. In a very loose and dangerously oversimplified way, it is possible to identify "being good" with being virtuous, and "doing bad" with the violation of the moral law. So that if it is possible for a good man to do a bad thing, it is because the development of a virtuous character is distinct from mere adherence to the moral law. Which of these is more fundamental? Is the development of virtues more important than adherence to duty, or is the moral law, being absolute, more deserving of our fundamental respect than the development of character? It would seem that if we affirm the latter, it is impossible for a good man to do a bad thing; whereas to affirm the former seems not only to allow for this, it seems to mute the stern authority of what is moral in order to make room for virtues to dominate. Because Lee possessed to a lofty degree the virtues of loyalty and nobility, as well as piety and courage, we soften the rigor of moral censure so that, without denying his moral error, we still call him good. Although it was morally wrong for him to have defended the evil institution supported by the Confederacy, his deep loyalty and devotion to Virginia redeems him from the censure of *being* bad merely because of his immoral (bad) action.

But this account is entirely unacceptable, for it seems to entail two separate and distinct notions of what it means to be good. To ask which of the two is more fundamental is to doom ethics to bipartisan strife. There is no doubt that there is a difference between an ethics based primarily on virtue and one based on morality, but to set them up as opposing candidates for supremacy is to transmogrify philosophy into politics. It is to avoid this quarrel that the question of whether a good man can do a bad thing is raised concretely. How do we think about this? From the previous reflections in this inquiry we have already learned much about what being good means by initiating the argument from the perspective of what it means to be bad. The three sources of being bad, misjudgment, weakness, and corruption remind us that to be good cannot mean to be perfect, for the perfect are impervious to all three sources. We do not always have perfect, apodictic knowledge about what we ought to do; but we are responsible for good judgment, which does not mean always assessing correctly. To be able to be tempted means that the moral law, though absolute and unchanging, is not in and of itself the origin of being good; rather, it is only in the struggle to achieve adherence to this law that we become good. And the corruption or ennoblement of our character depends upon the constant confrontation of our own development. These are not pleas for a less rigorous standard, as if by muting the severity of the absolute censure inherent in immoral action we simply make it easier to accommodate human frailty. Rather, this realization teaches us that being good *requires* the tension between virtue and morality. For this must be reiterated: the present inquiry does not seek to tell us, Moses-like, what commandments we ought to obey; rather it asks what it means to *be* good. That *being* virtuous and *doing* what is moral may at times seem to be in conflict merely reinforces the importance of judgment, strength, and character.

The question, therefore, becomes inverted: it is not whether a good man can do a bad thing, but whether being good *requires* being able to do a bad thing. The conflict, in other words, may be essential. The concrete is our anchor; and so we turn again to Lee. He loved his country. We call this patriotism, which is a kind of piety. To be pious is to revere as sacred what is our own, and, being sacred, is greater than our own individual selves. One cannot have piety for an abstraction, for we do not belong to abstractions, nor are they greater than us since we are the abstracting agent. Supreme piety is for the divine; but there is also communal piety or patriotism as well as familial piety. To say that piety is a virtue is to say (1) that to be pious is to learn to confront the greatness of that to which we belong, God or state or family; and (2) that to be pious is to excel; or to put it in other terms, it is better to be pious than to be impious or indifferent. It is this second characteristic that may be troubling. Is piety truly a virtue? If virtues are supposed to make us better, perhaps piety is not a virtue. Indeed, a strict moralist may reject the claim that piety, as a putative virtue, really does make us better. There is a long history in which nonpious critics have lamented the unnecessary suffering and bigotry laid at the doors of religious fervor or nationalism. Were it not far better not to revere God, king, country, or even family? Why not revere all men equally? Why revere anything?

Of course, reverence equally distributed is not reverence at all. The purely rational man, unfamilied, stateless and agnostic, bereft of all passion for a greatness that unifies, does not belong to anyone or anything. Why is such a man not as virtuous as a pious man? Because absolute individualism forfeits all possibility of love, sacrifice, forgiveness, and even wisdom. The impious may be gratified, intelligent, and knowledgeable but without reverence for greatness or the love of what unifies us as a people. They cannot be wise, for wisdom is not the possession of, but the love of, truth. Indeed, it is only because of Lee's ability to revere piously what he considered his homeland that any of his actions make any sense at all. But piety is necessary even for morality to make sense. For unless the moral law itself is revered, there is no compulsion to adhere to it save the sheer rationality of its formal structure. To submit to the authority of the moral law can be a form of piety, but only if it is revered as a power that unifies us. But this argument may seem to justify piety solely on the basis of its motivation for being *moral*, which is retrograde to the intent of the present argument. The point is not that piety is a virtue solely because it may motivate moral behavior; rather the point is to show how we think the interconnection between virtue and the moral law.

In Lee's case, however, it is precisely the conflict between his piety and improper behavior that is at issue. What is critical in this discussion is the difference between how we think of the virtuous man and how we think of the moral man. To act as a moral agent is to act willfully as we ought. To will is to act *as* a meaningful, judging agent. But to *be* a meaningful, judging agent is to have a developing character—that is, it must matter who we are and who we are becoming. Since character is developed by virtue, only those who have it can will to act morally. The temptation to reify the willful into a distinct metaphysical entity, the Will—capitalized—which becomes the *cause* of actions must be strenuously resisted. It is bad thinking. *We* act. There is not some inner force, identified as the Will, that acts, for that is the fallacy of mechanism, which is to explain the great by means of the small. It is true we act because we are willing beings, but that does not justify populating the universe with little Wills that lurk within larger persons. To act as a meaningful judging agent with a unique character, illuminated by virtue and darkened by vice, is to will. Keeping it in the verbal mode helps to avoid the mechanistic fallacy inherent in a substance metaphysics. The introduction of the term "Will" thus does not ease the tension, though it does draw our attention to why this problem is so thorny. Who I am must first *matter* before what I *do* can matter; yet what I do determines in part, though not exhaustively who I am. The question may be approached by variation of its form. Would we want there to be people like Robert E. Lee; or were it better had he never been born? This may seem an almost adolescent question, but it deserves consideration. Lee's piety and valor helped prolong a war that consumed thousands of lives and extended an unsavory rebellion. Yet it is difficult, perhaps impossible, to excise such magnificence from the pages of our history. We do not want the world to become entirely bereft of great and passionate character, nor are we willing even to concede that Lee's devotion to his own homeland is a bad thing in itself, even if we provisionally accept the account that it was this very passion that brought about so much immoral suffering. To hesitate to will that there be no more Robert Lees is revealing. It shows we assess the worth of the virtues independently of their contribution to moral behavior. There is more to being good than merely being moral, though to be immoral is always bad. There is likewise more to being bad than doing immoral acts. Perhaps, indeed, the guiding question of this chapter deserves an even more shocking formulation: perhaps *only* the good can do a bad thing. For only those who have character achieved through the learning virtues can act willfully, and only the willful can be bad. Those who are entirely corrupt, whose character is totally vicious, cannot act *willfully;* for they have neither judgment nor moral meaning. They might possibly be called evil—though that term is but a distraction here.

Is not the problem of Lee merely an epic representation of every one of us who care about who we are and what we ought to do? Is there not something so precious about our own character that rebellion on behalf of its sanctity, even if that rebellion is immoral, seems warranted? This is the dilemma we find in Genesis and reiterated in Milton's epic. Is not Eve precious to us because, in seeking to fulfill her destiny in confronting good and evil, she must violate the commandment forbidding her to be wise? Yet, to suggest this seems to condone license. It is to deny the very universality of the absolute, moral law; and this cannot be done.

Or, is it rather only *because* the moral law is absolute that the virtues, being independent of it, make us good? For we are neither absolute nor perfect; we are indeed finite and mortal, and if it is possible for us to be good rather than merely our actions being good, then what it means to be good must include our imperfections. To confront our imperfections is to be virtuous; to do what we ought is to be moral; to conjoin the virtuous with the moral is also good. But this conjunction is not correspondence or agreement, for what is finite cannot be in corresponding agreement with what is infinite. In this sense, piety, which is the reverential confrontation with the infinite, is the premier virtue, for it addresses the very essence of being true both to our character (who we are) and what we ought to do. Lee's great adversary, Abraham Lincoln, mirrors this anguish as well. Having sworn to uphold the Constitution, he violated it. He suspended the writ of habeas corpus long before Jefferson Davis did; he broke promises wantonly, and suppressed a free press, which the Confederacy never did. Yet, in saving the Union and in raising American oratory to the height of excellence, he somehow managed to show us who we truly are, and for these noble achievements he, too, is revered as a goodly man. We do not condone the actions of these men, at least not all of them. But it is the very actions we do not condone that seem to stand out as stemming from the remarkable virtues that these men seemed to possess to an extraordinary degree of excellence. If, however, the conjunction between virtue and morality cannot be corresponding agreement, then how are we to think of it? We have already seen that justice is thwarted by forgiveness, yet both are ways to be good. Is there a similarity here? Perhaps, but unlike forgiveness, this understanding must be sought in the threefold way in which we are good or bad: judgment, strength or weakness, and character. In exactly the same way I can judge well without having knowledge, or be tempted without being wicked, or learn to confront the infinite while still being finite, so, as virtuous I can revere what is moral even as I fail to live up to its rule. I cannot equate being good with doing only moral acts, for then only gods would be good, and temptation would be entirely eclipsed. Nor can I allow concern for my own excellence to outrank the universality of the moral law, for then I assume the mantle of divinity for my-self. If virtues be understood as ways of learning, that is, as ways of confronting our finitude in the reach for excellence, then the noncorrespondence with the absolute perfection of the moral law is at least thinkable.

But there are many virtues; and no one virtue suffices as a way of learning to excel, i.e., to reach for excellence. To be courageous must somehow interlock with what it means to be just, pious, wise, and noble. There is, of course, a great philosophical difficulty inherent in making sense of this interlocking. Plato struggles mightily with this problem in the *Protagoras,* and actually ranks the virtues in the *Republic;* though many scholars and critics do not seem to acknowledge the profundity of this problem as ad-dressed in these dialogues. Some see it merely as a definitional or conceptual puzzle. But the problem is far greater than that, and Plato knows it. How are we to think of justice and piety, loyalty to one but respect for all, as somehow producing a unitary way of being virtuous?

Lee is not only pious. In some ways he seems to represent most of the virtues in varying degrees. It is only because of this that he can be called virtuous; for if he were *only* pious or courageous he would not be deemed a good man. Perhaps this is because, as Plato suggests in the *Protagoras,* that truly to have one virtue is to have them all. But Lee's virtue must also entail respect for the moral law; for were he lacking in this respect we would not be able to call him good. So his violation of the moral law—if we insist on judging him so—stems not from a general indifference to morality but a continuing reverence for it even as he violates it. It must have been one of the most agonizing moments of his life when in 1861 Lincoln offered him the command of the Union army. He had been trained as an officer, after all, in that same army; had sworn an oath of allegiance to the United States, and had urged Virginia not to secede. Yet, there was never any real doubt: he could not draw his sword against what was his own. Though he may well have argued formally that union was morally preferable to secession, he judged—and that it was *judgment* and not mere preference or even "decision" is of extreme significance—that, given who he was, a son of Virginia, he would not abandon her. If we assume this willful act to have been immoral we must say he ought not to have done it. But, in making this judgment he embraced that very possibility—that he deserved the censure of doing what he ought not to have done. The reason why he can yet be judged good—and this judgment is *ours to* make under the assumptions we have provisionally accepted for this argument—seem to lie in two overlapping factors: that he was willing to accept the possibility of this censorious judgment; and that being *able* to judge depended on the very devotion he had toward his own belonging. Only as a son of Virginia was Lee, Lee. That is, only because he had become virtuous in the cultural origins of his homeland was he able to judge. To deny Virginia was to deny the very authorship of the judgment he made, even though it may have entailed the censure of immorality. And so the dreadful bind was this, that only by doing what may have been morally offensive could he willfully judge to honor what made him who he was.

This is, of course, neither a vindication nor an excuse. We are seeking to understand what it means to be good. The question is raised whether the good can ever do what is bad, aside form the obvious lapses or mistakes inherent in our humanity. If it is possible to affirm this, there must be both a difference and yet a powerful interdependence between virtue and morality. The difference is essential in order to allow the good to do what is bad; the interdependence is essential for the assignment of goodness. We are not here talking about conflicts *within* the moral, as if one were simply torn between two duties that seem to conflict, and one were trying to discover which duty was the true one. We are rather recognizing that the range of what it means to be good is not determined solely by the moral law. It is not compelling that Lee be judged an immoral man; just that he did an immoral thing.

Nevertheless, the mode of argumentation may appear misleading. By showing that respect, if not adherence, to the moral law is a prerequisite for being good it may seem that the inquiry must assume that the moral law is indeed the ultimate determiner of goodness. This, however, would be to misinterpret the argumentation. For the moral law itself follows from a judgment that being good matters. I *first* must care about being good before I can calculate, learn, or discover what is moral. Strictly speaking, not even "adherence" to the practice of the virtues, together with adherence to the moral law, can account for what it means to be good. It is rather the other way around. Being good—or at least being able to be good and caring about it—is what makes both the moral law and the virtues possible. The virtues, however many they may be, and the moral law, however derived, are necessarily serious concerns for the good; but they do not account for being good. They are, if you will, necessary but not sufficient conditions for being good, which is far more fundamental than either.

It may now be profitable to recast the original question. If it has been shown that a good man can do a bad thing, can a bad man do a good thing? At first it may seem that this question can only be given a negative answer, for if we are thoroughly corrupt, although we may accidentally perform beneficent actions, it seems a distortion of language to call anything good that proceeds from anyone who is bad. Of course it is not obvious that being bad means being totally corrupt any more than being good means being totally perfect. There seem to be three ways of being bad that not only can produce good actions but, when left to unfold themselves become ways of being good. If the analysis of these be correct, they deserve our present attention. And so we now focus on three figures: the rebel, the selfish (egotist), and the hater.

The Rebel. To rebel against the supreme authority, however it be conceived, God, the moral law, or even legitimate society, is to do what ought not to be done. Hence, to be a rebel, that is, to identify oneself as essentially irreverent of supreme authority is not only to perform an action prohibited by legitimate governance, it is to become outcast from the homeland to which one belongs, and is hence to *be* bad. And yet, in some cases, the rebel becomes so precious that as the scenario of the rebellion itself unfolds, the indictment becomes metamorphosed into sanction. Eve, in Milton's epic, is a rebel. She not only violates through disobedience the direct command of God, she even argues that such prohibitions are not binding because they keep her from achieving her complete independence. She thus judges her own existence above the law of God. She rebels. Her subsequent realization of her nudity and her acceptance of their expulsion from the garden shows that she herself judges her action to have deserved punishment. Yet, this act of rebellion and adoption of a rebellious character, which makes her undeserving of her proper dwelling, nevertheless purchases for her, and us, the very power or possibility of judging at all. As long as she remains docile and obedient she cannot judge; that is, she cannot think. For her to think *about* good and evil, which is what judging is, already exiles her from Eden. The actual eating of the fruit is symbolic only—to reflect on her own meaning *is* to possess the forbidden wisdom. Thus, the rebel, though bad because of disobedience, not only *does* a good thing—provides us with knowledge of good and evil—but *becomes* good, in a new sense of good, which means not mere adherence to the law, but one who risks the danger inherent in understanding the law.

All rebellion has this allure. It seeks autonomy. And only as autonomous can we matter. But only if we matter can we truly *be* good; because being able to be both good and bad alone makes being good worth the risk. The rebel may, therefore, as bad, achieve a making-possible of goodness. There is much that is paradoxical in this, but Milton's genius makes it compatible. The key to the unfolding of her rebellion is the discovery of her judgment. She is lured by Satan not to act, but to judge. Thus judgment entails risk. But only as risky is her existence meaningful.

Is it proper to say Eve is bad? Is she not good prior to her visit by the serpent? She is not good, but innocent, and as innocent, is incapable of *being* good. In rebelling against not only the command of God, but also her own happiness and belonging (to or in Eden) she is bad. In accepting her shameful nudity, however, she becomes, for the first time, able to be good. In achieving this power, sharing it lovingly with Adam, and enduring her own exile, she becomes good. Thus, a bad person can do a good thing. This is not to say that rebellion always achieves being good. Most acts of rebellion are not only immoral, they also corrupt character. But to be able to rebel protects that precious, ultimate independence the lack of which makes risk, and hence judgment, impossible. It is the truth of this, and not its incitement to rebellion as a way of life, that matters. After Eden, when Eve was good, she was no longer rebellious. That this is both enigmatic and paradoxical is obvious. That further analysis is needed in subsequent chapters of this troubling truth is no less so.

The Proud. Those who are selfish and egotistical have long been recognized as failing to qualify as being good, and the reasons for this are obvious. The selfish by definition rank their own gratification and esteem above all else, including the moral law. To be utterly selfish is contemptible, for it cancels all possibility of kindness, sympathy, understanding, love, and sacrifice. In children it produces spoiled brats, in adults the insufferably arrogant, in rulers, despotic tyrants. As long as this self-centeredness is petty and vulgar, little benefit can come of it.

But in a curious way, supreme selfishness can become a kind of pride, that, though originally vile and immoral, can provide a certain esteem of one's own worth such that pettiness itself can no longer be endured. This is the kind of analysis that Nietzsche uncovers in *Toward a Genealogy of Morals,* identifying those he clepes as "noble" to be so assured of their own superiority that they actually *become* superior. Always capable of disdain and contempt, they eschew the disdainful and contemptuous in themselves. The realization is thereby developed that all meanness of spirit is unworthy of them. From simple arrogance, which is a vice, they develop self-esteem, which is a virtue. But more than that, in maintaining a sense of personal superiority they curiously subvert their own egotism into the notion of excellence in itself, creating not a personal but a moral superiority. It becomes clear to them that to claim superiority on the basis of deceit connotes not superiority but inferiority, and so the deceit itself must be forsworn. The prideful become proud. And one can become too proud to be base.

This seems to happen occasionally in political histories, when a ruthless effort to achieve a lofty office is followed by a stunning reversal in character once the position is secured. We sometimes speak of the "office making the man"; but it may simply be that the arrogance of the campaign is translated into a pride of command. Even in cases where the arrogance remains a vice, the proud resistance against what is good strikes us as curiously admirable. When Don Giovanni, in Mozart's supreme opera, refuses to recant even as he is swallowed up into the eternal fires of hell, the music as well as the boldness of his character retains no little respect for the villainous but steadfast Don. The uneasy judgment we make at opera's end is testimony once again to the worth we attribute to the autonomy of spirit. Mozart's libretto puts the Don in Hell; assessment of his cruel and selfish violations of the moral law likewise indicts him; but Mozart's music, through which we glean insights into the strength of his character, troubles the judgment. Pride itself deserves further reflection. In some cases, however, it is clear that the selfish can develop into a pride that redeems (Goethe's Faust?), and so there seems at least another sample of the bad doing what is good.

The Hater. In Aeschylus's *Oresteia,* hate seems to follow hate in a fuliginous descent into an endless series of answered wrongs. The black despair of ceaseless vengeance consumes the entire house of Atreus. Only in the third and final drama is the hideous cycle eased, and that is accomplished only by divine intervention. But this stygian passion of vengeful hatred began long before the first play, *Agamemnon.* Thyestes seduces his brother's wife; in revenge, Atreus tricks his cuckolding brother into eating his own children. Thyestes curses his brother's entire house; his one remaining son, Aegisthus later seduces Clytemnestra, the wife of Atreus's son, Agamemnon. She hates her husband, Agamemnon for sacrificing her beloved daughter, Iphigenia, and so on his return, supported by her lover Aegisthus, murders him in the intimacy of his bath. Agamemnon's remaining children, Orestes and Electra, now hate their mother, and kill both her and Aegisthus. The furies then seek vengeance on Orestes, but Athena judges in his favor, and the mad cycle of hatred and vengeance is finally over. Even this brief summary seems to overwhelm us with its senseless and unremitting despair. So much hate, passing through three generations, like primeval Montagues and Capulets, causing so much suffering, deceit, wickedness and passion, indicts the entire cast as unworthy killers.

And yet it is the genius of Aeschylus that reveals to us something far deeper than this pendulation from one wrong to another that constitutes the indictment of the events. For when the seeker after vengeance confronts the dread wrong done to one's beloved, the ensuing passion seems justified. For what is a mother who will not avenge her daughter's death? Or a son who will leave unanswered his father's murder? In *Agamemnon* there is something magnificent about Clytemnestra; for her obligation to Iphigenia reverberates as a mother's solemn duty to hate the slayer of her child. Hate is the spawn of justice. In *The Libation Bearers* the brother and sister must honor their murdered father. The injustice of his homicide shrieks out at us through the magnificence of the Aeschylean poetry; we sense the inner rightness of the children's plotting. They are not as magnificent as their mother, perhaps; but their devotion to Agamemnon and the terrible wrong they alone can answer compels us to revere the passion for matricide. On the personal level, is not hate often necessary to compel the otherwise wavering spirit to retribute great wrong? The passions, that in their consequence blacken the pages of such dread chronicles, are, in their origins, of brighter hue. To be a hater is to soil one's own existence with the darkest grime; but to hate what is hateful can yield what is good. The journey through these ugly responses of passionate haters, when confronted in such revealing art, illustrates this curious education. Hate can justify. Haters can answer a hateful wrong. The corrupt can achieve a moral end.

The three ways in which the bad can achieve the good have their origins in the three ways of being bad discovered in the initiation of the inquiry: bad judgment, weakness, and corruption. The rebel becomes rebellious in being able to judge; the weakness of selfishness becomes the strength of pride; the corruption of the hater inspires the outrage of the just. These are not mere scenarios of bad people becoming good, for that is neither unusual nor remarkable. Rather, these accounts show that what it means to be bad or good outranks the labels of the moral and the virtuous. But this seems to bring us back to our first confrontation. Is not Antony's outrage at Caesar's murder akin to the outrage of Atreus's blighted family? The inquiry seems to have come full circle, suggesting perhaps that the indirect approach of considering what it means to be bad offers no further purchase. It is an uneasy venture to suggest that the good, as good, can do what is bad; or even that the bad, as bad, can do what is good. It were easier, perhaps, if, through subtle redefinition we manage to show that the moral must always march step by step with the virtuous, that being bad is always doing bad, and no ethical space exists outside the absolute precepts of the moral law. It is not only uneasy to deny this, it is uncomfortable in the extreme: perhaps it is even dangerous. The question, however, is always this: is it true? If it is true, our very being is a risk.

Perhaps a better example can be found in a more amiable character that appeals on a more fundamental level. When Huckleberry Finn was forced to confront the dilemma inherent in setting his friend Jim free, he reasoned in a remarkable way. The moral law, at least as he thought he knew it, the law that those he admired and even those he loved assured him was right, told him that Jim, as a slave, belonged to Tom Sawyer's Aunt Polly. He had no reason to doubt the validity of that law. And so he faced it directly. It was bad to set Jim free; and he would be punished in hell for doing it. There was no doubt here, no fancy redefining, no escape. But Jim was his friend. "Well, I'll go to hell, then." We cannot simply leave it as boyish naiveté. Huck is a good boy doing what is, to his lights, a bad thing. Since he thought it was wrong, he was bad in doing it. There is the terrible burden of judgment here; there is the balance between strength and weakness; and there is character. The novelist, Rex Stout, suggests that this is the most important sentence in American literature; he may be right. To confront the truth inherent in what this judgment and what this character means cannot be avoided. It is this dread confrontation that requires the kinds of distinctions that this transitional chapter considers. The question, what does it mean to be good, cannot escape the need to make Huckleberry Finn's dilemma intelligible. It is only because a good boy, like Huck, can do a bad thing, that ethical truth matters more than ethical behavior.

Part Three

What It Means to Be Good

8

The First Way of Being Good: Judgment

We judge when we do not know. If judgment is what we do in the absence of certain knowledge, then who we are must play a role in judging that is lacking in knowledge. To judge that the soufflé is done is part of what makes a great chef; but to know that three teaspoons make a tablespoon, though far more certain and hence communicable to apprentice cooks, does not make one a chef at all. Knowledge claims are in principle both communicable and repeatable; they are independent of any particularizing quality of the knower, for we do not care *who* makes the claim that sugar dissolves in water, but we do care that is was Hannibal's judgment to cross the Alps or Chamberlain's judgment to sign the Munich agreement with Hitler, or Mozart's judgment to introduce the great duet with Papageno's stutter. Thus, to judge is to become a unique and determining part of the synthesizing that brings the elements together into a cohesive whole.

In the present context we restrict ourselves solely to those judgments the making of which enables us to be good. This is not merely to make a moral claim; for to assert that one ought to keep one's promises, which is a moral claim, is not a judgment, for it does not need a particular and unique judge to make it. To judge that we shall indeed keep this promise, in spite of the fact that to do so entails the sacrificial loss of what is greatly precious, reveals that how we are, as judges who are willing to endure this loss, matters. Thus, to be able to judge cannot be accounted for by understanding how we make knowledge claims or even moral claims.

This is not a deficiency, as if it were better always to have knowledge and thus never to need to judge. Indeed, to be able to judge provides the possibility of contributing to the cohesive synthesis in a way that makes who we are as judges matter. To be able to matter would entirely be forfeit were only knowledge or the certainty of moral claims possible. It is Hannibal who matters in the judgment to cross the Alps; the mere knowledge claim that African elephants can be led across such perilous terrain leaves out the very boldness and uniqueness of Hannibal, which historically made the crossing possible. To judge not only requires the uniqueness of a particular judge, it also changes the judge himself. It is only those cases in which the change on the judge is to his betterment that concerns this inquiry. To judge in such a way as to become good by the making of the judgment is what matters here. Thus we must distinguish a moral *claim* (it is wrong to break a promise) from a moral *judgment* (I hereby fulfill the promise in spite of the suffering involved in keeping it.)

It cannot be that only proper judgments make us good; that is, *it is not the making of good judgments but the good making of judgments* that is important. It is certainly possible for one who is good to make a judgment well that turns out to be bad or false. And it is also possible to make a good judgment badly. Thus it is not the content or even the result of a judgment that makes us good. How, then are we to understand this?

If the making of a judgment necessarily includes the quality of the judge—as it *must,* since in the absence of complete knowledge what provides the cohesion is the contribution inherent in what it means to judge at all—then it is how this factor of *being* the judge contributes to the judgment that determines the *making* of it as good or bad. We say we judge precisely in those cases in which the synthetic cohesion—how the pieces fit together—are not all provided by direct knowledge. In other words, we must contribute our own reading of the various elements. Since who we are therefore becomes essential for the judgment to occur, and since what makes it necessary to judge is the lack of knowledge, then it is how we confront our own ignorance that makes the cohesion possible.

We can provisionally identify this confrontation of our own ignorance necessary for making judgments either as wisdom or foolishness. But this does *not* mean that our confrontation with our ignorance is wise if the judgment turns out to be correct nor foolish if
it turns out to be incorrect. When the nature of the judgment
has moral significance—which is the only kind that concerns us
here—our own involvement in it as confronters of our ignorance
alone makes us good.

To confront our ignorance well is wisdom; to confront it badly or
not to confront it at all, is foolishness. What does it mean to confront our ignorance well? At the very least, it is to recognize ignorance *as* ignorance, for not to recognize our ignorance as ignorance is to beguile ourselves—that is, it is to be foolish.

Yet this acceptance of ignorance as ignorance is not sufficient.
We must also accept the *need* to judge; we should not, out of fear
of misjudgment, simply refuse to judge at all. There is boldness in
Hannibal's judgment to venture over the Alps to attack Rome, a
boldness that entails a risk. What is crucial here is the realization
that one's own self is an actual ingredient in the mosaic of judgment. What allows our judging to be a resource of our own being
good is that our own reading and hence synthesizing embraces the
limits of our being ignorant together with the need to risk our own
involvement.

In the previous sketch of comedic folly, it was discovered that
judgment is always of oneself in terms of how and where we fit into
the world. To misread one's position in the world is either the denial of one's ignorance, which makes us arrogant and hence *silly*,
or *open* to one's ignorance, which makes us amazed at our own
dislocation, and hence comically *foolish* and thus ready to be made
wise. To read our own ignorance, and hence possible foolishness,
as lessons from which we gain enlightenment is wisdom—but always a wisdom seeded in our own folly. It is for this reason that the
virtues, of which wisdom is the one by which we judge ourselves in
the world, must always be seen as learnings, not as the achieved
good. We learn to confront our ignorance in our judgments about
our being in the world, and this *learning* is wisdom. This learning
is not the achievement of knowledge, but it is to become who we
are. Wisdom is therefore never to be equated with the success or
rightness of the judgment, and certainly not the acquisition of

knowledge. To try to achieve a synthetic cohesion and not include ourselves is therefore a distortion of the judgment and is hence, a kind of unwisdom that is silliness.

In the *First Part* we noted that one of the three ways of being bad is manifested in the ghastly utterance "How could I have been so stupid?" This self-censure is not made when an important judgment turns out to be false. It is made only when a judgment is *badly made,* not when the judgment is bad. Thus even a judgment that turns out to be bad or false can, if not badly made, still make us good. For our embrace of our own ignorance, wedded to the painful enlightenment found in the learning of the harsh lesson, prohibits us from the ghastly self-censure earned by a judgment badly made. Indeed, if we seek to censure ourselves unduly for a wrong judgment well made, we engage in a self-eclipsing arrogance that is silly and puritanical. Under the influence of such silliness we cannot learn. To be able to learn, after all, is the basis of all the virtues.

To judge locates us in the world; it shows we belong in the world, and hence we are not somehow outside the world, appraising it as an external object. To judge morally makes this location matter. To belong to the world as mattering is one of the fundamental ways of being able to be good, which is concretized in the making of a moral judgment. To make a judgment badly is to upset the possibility of learning what it means to be in the world as a judge. Being able to judge morally is prior to any action, not merely in a temporal sense, but in a formal sense as well. To judge myself unfettered by a prior and binding promise not only precedes the immoral act of breaking the promise, it is what constitutes the possibility of being responsible for the violation. Such judging distorts my belonging in the world; it is a misreading of the mosaic of interlocking elements. It is not that I am uninformed of the promise's binding influence, or even that I have forgotten what it means to promise, for these may possibly excuse. It is rather that, in making the judgment that the promise does not bind me, I am misreading the elements that must fit together, one of which is my own belonging in the world as a judge. To distort the cohesion so as to make it incoherent is made possible by my *being* the judge. There is no prior faculty that accounts for this, for if there were, my role as judge would be lost, i.e., it would be subsumed under this higher principle. To be good, therefore, is to retain not only my own status as the interpreter of the elements, but to allow—or "make"—these elements (which includes myself) fit together. This "fitting together" however, is not merely a rational testing of consistency, an error often made by purely formalist accounts. It is rather to read the pieces as belonging together, however broadly that is conceived.

To ask whether this misreading is *deliberate* is to interpose a prior faculty of agency or will, which totally vexes the entire description. For if there need be some prior metaphysical power that *precedes* the judging, then there is no judgment *at all.* Metaphysical entities conceived as *causes* of this judging, such as the Will, or metaphysical notions such as "agency" or "freedom" are not only unnecessary at this stage, they are distractions. Once it is understood that we do indeed make moral judgments, and that this locates us within the world as a part of what is brought together, the need for free agency as a prior metaphysical cause is no more defensible than determinism. What matters is simply that we judge, and who or what this "we" is can be found only in the judging itself. For the key to such notions as freedom, agency, and responsibility is simply that in moral judging we always judge ourselves.

To judge morally is therefore to *become* who we are; it is not only to *assemble* the parts into a cohesive whole, but to *become a part* of the assemblage. To judge badly is to fail at this cohesion and hence to be bad; to judge well is to place oneself properly within the mosaic of elements, and hence is to be good. One way to be good, therefore, is to become who we are by putting ourselves coherently in the world; i.e., it is to judge ourselves. Since *we* do the judging we are never entirely eclipsed by the greater cohesion that is the world; but since, in *moral* judgments we are also a *part* of that greater cohesion, neither are we ever entirely the determiners. We neither make up our own morality (which is silliness) nor do we disappear into a mechanistic tyranny of the inevitable (which is nihilistic.) The awareness of this truth is not to be found in the postulation of dubious metaphysical entities like the free will, but in the concrete unpacking of our own being able to judge.

We are asking not what actions ought to be done—an entirely legitimate but derived question—but what it means to be good. We have recognized there is more than one way to be good, but that one of the ways to be good is to judge ourselves, which means: to *belong* in the world, in such a way that this belonging is as a judge. The cohesion, or bringing-together of the elements cannot, then, be the mere connection of concepts (as Kant defines it), and certainly it cannot be the logical or formal connections of propositions, or even sentences. The "elements" that make up the mosaic are primarily ways of being, though they may also include situations, prior events, and contract-like understandings or commitments.

In order to "bring together" such existential elements, there must be some confrontation of the whole—usually understood as the world—in which the various elements are read as belonging together. Thus the essence of judgmental cohesion is the whole outranking the parts. It is therefore exactly the opposite of mechanism that explains larger things in terms of smaller things, whereas judgment explains smaller things in terms of larger ones. To judge oneself as a son owing allegiance to one's father is to read "being a son" in terms of the broader "being a family." To judge badly in this case would reverse the process, judging the family in terms of being the son, which is not only disruptive of the cohesion but also impious. Thus, to be good is to belong within the whole—which requires a reading of the whole—and to be bad is to fragment one's belonging so that the parts become unintelligible by their noncohesion.

This notion of reading the parts, including oneself, in terms of the whole cannot be understood as a purely intellectual endeavor, for the self that belongs is not mere mind. To resist being fragmented, and hence to belong to a unifying synthesis, is integrity, that is: keeping oneself intact. Thus to be good as judging is to integrate oneself not only within the greater whole (piety) but also to belong as the judging element that matters (integrity). Since this judging also must confront our ignorance, the acceptance of our finitude (modesty, humility, or what the Greeks call *sophrosone*) is also necessary. Yet, this confrontation should not intimidate us into not judging at all, so a certain respect for oneself as daring to take the risk (pride) also matters. It can thus be seen that many traditional virtues are inherent in the concrete understanding of judging.

But the fundamental, and hence most significant aspect of how judging contributes to being good is the ability to *be read* in light of the greater whole. This is not to speak of judging, but of *being* judged by the judge that is oneself. We are not only readers (as judges) but we are also *read*. Yet, we are not texts, nor phenomena being interpreted by some external observer, such as a sociologist, but elements within a cohesive mosaic that, *as* read, interlocks with other elements. What it means to be good is thus to be able to be read in such a way that we belong *as* both judge and judged in a cohesive whole. To see oneself in terms of the wider scope in which we belong as see-ers is thus presupposed when, for example, we read ourselves within the unfolding story of belonging, so that the hungry are fed, the wretched comforted, the weak supported. It is *not* because the hungry have *rights;* or even that I have a *duty* to feed them; but rather that both rights and duties follow from the shared belonging in the world where I am both judge and judged.

There is, nevertheless, a far more revealing phenomenon inherent in judging that occasionally becomes dominate in our confrontation with out own ignorance, and this is trust. For when we deal with others, or even ourselves, we must submit our own ignorance either to trust or mistrust. For if natural phenomena are never completely known, far more uncertain are the complex levels of human guile and innocence. Trust is a virtue only if it is not reduced to naiveté; mistrust is not a vice unless it is reduced to base suspicion. The differences cannot be determined by reliance on what is *known,* for the reason trust is revered as a virtue is because we do *not* know. There is no trust when one is certain.

Why, then, is trust a virtue? It is, in a way, a yielding of certainty or at least personal control for the sake of another's possibility for integrity. In trust, we allow another to manifest his integrity; and this allowance is a judgment, the very making of which honors the trusted. Trust is sacrificial: we yield the reliable, which is dear, for the sake of another, as precious. This celebrates our ignorance, for were I certain, I could not trust; and trust, as a virtue, is a way of learning to be who we are as being good.

Trust is almost paradigmatically judgmental; yet it is both elusive and subtle. We prefer sentries and courts, policemen and warriors to be mistrustful—for caution, as a kind of prudence, can also be virtuous. To be naive is a vice; indeed naiveté is more of a nonjudgment than a misjudgment. Strictly speaking, therefore, we cannot be "too trusting"—although in ordinary language it is a perfectly legitimate locution—for trust, as a virtue, is an acceptance of our own ignorance about another's reliability. Naiveté, or "being overly trustful," is simply to disregard our ignorance—or worse: to be unaware of it. The beauty of trust is therefore the sacrificial risk taken on behalf of another's fidelity, which celebrates our ignorance by confronting our finitude nobly. Although I use the term "another," strictly speaking this is too narrow, since obviously I can either trust or mistrust myself as well.

Prudence—as a kind of mistrust—is also a virtue dependent upon judgment. To be able to distinguish when we should trust and when, or whom, to mistrust prudently is obviously a mark of wisdom. Yet simple mistrust by itself is not only unwise, it is often a form of self-deceit. A curious but revealing example offers itself.

René Descartes, in the First Meditation, introduces what he calls "methodic doubt." This is often interpreted as a kind of skepticism; indeed some critics have tried to push this approach into a radical position leading to total nihilism. And perhaps, in some senses, Descartes is vulnerable to such reductionism. But when his position is viewed critically, Descartes is surely the most trusting—perhaps even to the point of naiveté—thinker who ever wrote. For he trusts absolutely in his *method*. The outrage is that, *prior* to his deliberations, he has total faith that the "method of doubting"—which he himself never *doubts* at all—will lead him to absolute, certain knowledge. Talk about *trust!* Believing *beforehand* in a *method,* and indeed a method of *doubting,* is almost comical. There are many philosophers who rather arrogantly maintain they have resolved some or even all of the great philosophical questions; but they base these assessments on what they have accomplished in their inquiries. Descartes, however, assures us he will be right even before he knows what the inquiry will produce: he *trusts absolutely* the method itself. It's bad enough to adopt sufficient arrogance after an impressive work has been carried out; but to adopt this posture solely on the basis of a blind trust in a method is ridiculous.

The point is, "absolute trust" is simply self-contradictory. To trust is to be finite. It is one of the ways (called "virtues") by which we learn to confront our finitude. God cannot trust. To ask: how do we *know* when to trust? is as silly as Descartes' blind trust in doubting. We obviously cannot *know* when or whom to trust, for the knowledge would forfeit the trusting. Nevertheless, it is absurd to argue that all trusting, since it is bereft of certainty, is equally virtuous. It is a matter of judgment.

In a rational sense, doubting is no more and no less reasonable than believing, for both belief and doubt are equal, possible responses to our ignorance. To doubt the existence of the midnight sun simply because it has not been directly experienced is as absurd as believing in werewolves and vampires simply because they make for good stories. We have reasons for believing and reasons for doubting, just as there are reasons for trusting and for mistrusting. Not all of these reasons are evidentiary; indeed some of these reasons are compelling even when no evidence can be called upon in support. We do not indict ourselves of irrationality if our beliefs were strongly supported by both good reasons and evidence, but turned out to be false. Indeed, to doubt or to mistrust in the face of evidence or reasoned belief is less rational than to accept on trust.

But trust seems somehow more personal than belief. I believe that certain claims are true; I believe that certain things that I have not experienced, exist. But it seems I *trust* people.

And here we must return, briefly, to Othello. He did not trust Desdemona. As was noted, mistrust is a vice only when it becomes base. Is not marriage a commitment not only to be faithful, i.e., trustworthy, but also *to trust?* Does not Othello owe his wife sufficient trust as to resist the lure of jealousy? To be sure, Iago's guile and cunning is skillful; and the audience may think Othello has been given enough tainted evidence to make continued trust mere blindness. But of course we realize, upon reflection, that Iago's evidence—the dropped handkerchief—is minimal. He does not probe Othello's *doubts,* but his very trust. The cleverness lies in Iago's making Othello doubt, not Desdemona, but Othello's own trusting. He mistrusts his own trust. We, the audience, realize this when Othello discovers his own mistrust in the final act. He does not blame Iago, but himself. It is not that Iago made him doubt; it is that his doubting, his mistrust, had become *base* or ignoble. As ignoble as dirt.

Trust is therefore a virtue precisely because it embraces our finitude. To judge is also to embrace our own lack of omniscience. We see that it is possible to succeed or fail in making judgments, not because the judgment itself is false, but because the *making* of it is distorted. Hence, one way to be good is to judge well.

9

The Second Way of Being Good: Moral Strength

It is perhaps among the most curious—not to say strangest—of all human phenomena. We risk our own security and happiness for the sake of something (or someone) apparently other than ourselves, often on behalf of the ephemeral, like honor, or the abstract and distant, like a principle. We sometimes sacrifice even for an unworthy thing, an eggshell as Hamlet says, and think it good. It seems at first glance entirely strange; for why should we willfully suffer, shed blood, perhaps even die, for anything at all, ever?

And yet it is at the same time profoundly familiar. Whether we seem bereft of all its vestiges, or are abundantly bestowed, we know what it means to be called upon to hazard our person and our pleasures. Courage is an early word, learned young, ample in its treasury, told in a thousand stories, and revered in the annals of our heritage. As children, even if we cannot be said to know, we nevertheless are assured of the truth that sacrifice is noble, that courage is radiant, that a life measured solely by its length falls short, but a life shortened by honor has reached its fullest measure. It is thus both strange and familiar, so blatant it is grasped by children, yet so subtle it escapes captive assurance even by the sagest of the sage. It may be that all great and fundamental notions are like this, we are familiar with them, but they evade the probing of our lamps.

Moral strength, sometimes thought of as courage, is perhaps impossible to anatomize precisely because, as fundamental, it cannot be dissected into parts or explained in terms more basic than itself. The error, then, which makes the quest seem hopeless, is to seek for some faculty, cause, or psychological condition that accounts for the phenomenon. It is likewise futile to search for courage in the notion of agency, as was noted earlier in the reflections on temptation. But if these accustomed and pretraveled routes are closed to us, how can we proceed? Though it may be impossible to analyze moral strength as if it were made up of more fundamental elements, it is not thereby rendered totally inaccessible. The question then is not what courage is, but rather what it means to be courageous or to be morally strong.

The first step in this realization of meaning is to divorce the worth of courage from its accustomed union to the implementation of the moral law. This separation suggests that courage is not merely a means of achieving something else that is good—the morally right action—but that courage is intrinsic in its worth. When the old man, Nono, in Williams's play *Night of the Iguana* pleads with the gods, he asks:

> Oh courage, could you not as well
> Select a second place to dwell?
> Not only in that golden tree
> But in the frightened heart of me?

The poet does not ask to *succeed* in the enterprise, but simply to confront it courageously. Indeed, since it is possible to succeed without courage, as well as to fail with it, then to pray for courage is to esteem it independently of the worth of the victory. Thus to understand courage requires more than its service on behalf of doing what is right. But what does this mean? Courageously to confront a task regardless of its outcome, means that, although the success matters greatly, to emerge from the struggle with our own worth intact is greater. It is to reach out beyond the mere calculus of success, and to register as significant what it means to confront it at all.

To pray for courage is itself an act of courage, for of all the virtues, it alone must always be unpleasant. There is no courage without fear, stress, and pain; so to ask to *be* courageous is to invite a torment that might possibly be avoided by the craven. This is not a perverse seeking out of misery for its own sake, but a willingness to confront our troubles rather than to be anaesthetized against their pain. It is this realization that is so illuminating. For, in praying for courage rather than success, we care about our own integrity as a meaningful element in the forthcoming struggle. To pray that we should *not* have to confront the struggle at all, that to win or lose should occur by accident, or by forces other than ourselves, is to hope that *we* are not needed at all. It is thus possible to hope or pray for success without hoping or praying for the courage to play a role in the struggle. If being courageous is a way of being good, then, it must be because who we are, as a necessary element in the trouble that impends, matters as much as, or even more than, success. So; to be good must mean to be a part of struggles that matter, in which we must *care* for success but not *rely* on it for our moral worth. The craven, too, want success; but they do not want themselves to matter as a part of that success, not merely because they fear unsuccess (since both the courageous and the cowardly do this), but because they also fear the effort. They do not confront either of these two fears, but seek a narcotic or a numbing of their sensibilities so as not to feel the fear at all.

This isolation of courage from the mere service of moral action reinforces the earlier drawn distinction between being good and being moral. However, care must be taken with the logic inherent in this distinction. Although courage may be a virtue independently of its service on behalf of moral action, it is not possible courageously to be bad. Obviously one can *bravely* perform immoral acts, and can even *courageously* fail to perform moral acts; but one cannot *courageously* will to perform immoral acts. The truth of these claims does not entail that the worth of courage lies solely in the supportive role it plays in adherence to the moral law. It may take great courage to confront a weakness even if the result is once again to succumb to it; but it cannot be courageous blindly to confront a situation in which failure is inevitable or even willed. There is an existential risk in courage, but it is a risk worth taking simply because in taking it the integrity of our existence is at stake.

Courage seems to require some sense of a greatness or a meaning that transcends mere individual satisfaction or personal triumph. It is usually, though not always, grounded in a transcending institution such as a beloved country, family, or religion for which, and in behalf of which, one sacrifices private interest, the way a courageous soldier dies for his country, or a martyr sacrifices his life for a belief. To be courageous is to judge who one is in terms of belonging, for sacrifice is never made merely for private advantage (for that is mere prudential engineering). There must, in courageous sacrifice, be some offering of what is endured for the sake of some greater reality, the participation in which amplifies our worth or even extends the dimensions that establish how we think about who we are. In spite of this appeal to the greater reality, however, courage is always a form of self-esteem, a reluctance to shrink in the measure of one's self by one's self. There is, therefore, always a kind of gentle but ineluctable paradox in courage: the sacrifice of one's own private advantage for the sake of the greater institution or principle that is revered in the offering oddly does not result in the diminishment of one's existential worth but in the expansion of it. It might be seen as a kind of pride, in which one's refusal to be diminished is accomplished by diminishing one's interests or advantage.

These caveats against judging courage merely as a condition for achieving morally good actions, though important, do not suffice to tell us what it means to have moral strength. Nor does the warning to avoid reducing moral strength to a metaphysical cause or agency relieve us of the further toil needed to think properly about this way of being good. For one thing, to shift from the term "courage" to the phrase "moral strength" focuses on a hitherto untouched aspect of the phenomenon, namely that strength is acquired. If this be so, then the current of this acquisition itself becomes a part of our understanding what it means. We should perhaps distinguish provisionally between strength and power. An enormous boulder teetering on the edge of a cliff, or a thundering heard of frightened buffalo suggests power, but a colt running across the field suggests a strengthening of legs not yet the caliber of a thoroughbred. To empower a regiment to act by the command of the officer is to release the energy already there; to strengthen the muscles of the gymnast is to tighten and tone through discipline the limbs of a future Olympian. This subtle but essential distinction is important, for we do not wish to speak of moral power (which might be the same as a sufficient causal agency), but of that which is achieved through strengthening. Just as a strong muscle is appreciated not only because of what it may do, but also because of the exercise and training that brings it to its performative edge, so in the moral realm, it is not the mere potency to act that matters, but the regime of training that its precedent story provides that in part constitutes its worth. In this sense, power is given and hence is mine only by possession, strength is achieved and hence is mine by dint of earning and sacrifice. The training that strengthens morally is learning.

The metaphoric isomorphism between achieved physical strength and learned moral strength is used with great effect by Plato in the *Republic*. The education of the guardians or warriors is shown to be twofold: gymnastic and musical, from the Greek *gumnos*, meaning naked; and *musike*, that bestowed by the muses. Just as hard, physical training produces beauty (*kalos*) in the naked body, so education in the various arts produces nobility (*kalos*) in the soul. In neither of these cases is utility or effectiveness the sole or even determining factor; rather it is the beauty or nobility inherent in the training or achievement that counts primordially.

Moral strength is what it is because of moral strengthening. It is not a natural gift like a powerful bone-structure, but an achieved and disciplined accomplishment by which the natural gift is refined to a radiant excellence. The fact that Plato's account of this moral and physical training of the guardians is meant, in the dialogue, to show us what *courage* means, is of no small matter. For courage consists, as Socrates contends in the metaphor of the dog, of *learning* to see the good, not as private advantage, as do the citizens, but as good in itself. We must be *taught* to judge the good as universal.

For Plato, therefore, the meaning of courage is two-fold: it is that which alone allows us to *grow* from seeking benefit to seeking goodness itself; and it is *learned* from a participation in and reverence for a cultural reality that exceeds in importance that of the private reality. One can no more divorce learning from being courageous than one can sever the development of a story from its conclusion. Learning is therefore not the mere means to achieve the end, courage, but is an essential and fundamental part of the virtue. For Socrates in the dialogue, the telling characteristic of courage is the shift from goodness as advantage to goodness as intrinsic. This ability to recognize the differences and to prefer the intrinsic over the extrinsic is seen as a kind of achieved strength that only a cultural *polis* can provide. Without this spiritual learning, the hegemony of personal interest could never be overcome, for the youth would never be able to *think* there ever could be such a thing as being good just for the sake of being good and not for some personal advantage; and furthermore, even if he could somehow grasp such a notion, he would not be strong enough to extract himself from the lures of interest.

But if moral strength is a kind of learning (and not merely the *result* of learning) then it seems that moral weakness would be the cessation of learning, or at least a derailing of the journey, as in distraction. We become distracted and hence weak not because of bad learning but because we stop learning altogether. Strictly speaking, therefore, we should not really speak of moral strength as the second way of being good, but moral strengthening, so that the emphasis is placed upon the continuing process of learning who we are.

Nevertheless, the Platonic focus seems to be that only through such learning is it possible to shift the focus from goodness seen as personal advantage to goodness in itself, a shift that seems echoed in ordinary, everyday thinking about courage. For to be courageous usually seems to entail a sacrifice of personal interest or security on behalf of the nobler or intrinsic sense of who we are. To say it takes courage to enter a burning building to save a child is to say in confronting the fear of our own being burned we become *good* and not merely *satisfied* in such effort. What justifies the risk is becoming good simply for the sake of being good. The particular is risked in the confrontation of fear for the sake of the universal.

Moral weakness is therefore a species of personal diminishment, a shrinking of the range of who we are. It is to become a sham, a fake, a veneer of humanity rather than the solid wood. This diminishing of oneself results from distraction from one's true self. Thus, moral strength is a species of concentration, by which the lures of derailment or distraction are resisted by the sheer strength of the

growing, widening reality of our becoming. It is not so much that
we "are" universal, but that we approach it through a learning that
can be distracted by particularity and furthered by growing strength.
Thus as courageous we can pray for courage just because this virtue directs our growing toward the nobler, or more universal. To be
good is thus to approach the greatness in universality. But this is
not abstract, person-eclipsing universal, as if we become clones of
the same originary stamp; it is on the contrary an intensification of
uniqueness, a celebration of one's own special meaning. We are
aware of this because of the way in which the craven seek diminishment of themselves and the courageous confront the significance of themselves in the struggle for success.

But if Plato is correct in his insight that the virtue of courage is
linked to the learning of the good for its own sake (*ton agathon
auton*), then this learning cannot be a mere acquisition of knowledge nor accumulation of mere facts. Rather, to learn is to become
who we are. Learning as becoming or growing rather than as ac-
quisitive or possessive is the foundation for the good life. Informational possession need not better or enhance our life; indeed a
sheer encyclopedic access to information itself can be a distraction
from true learning and hence from becoming courageous. This becomes clear when the translation is guided by a passion for truth:
we do not seek "goodness" as an abstraction, but to become good
simply for the sake of *being* good. This "seeking" or "learning" to
become good just for its own sake is courage. It is not merely inci-
dental that this teaching is consistent with the Socratic equation of
virtue with wisdom and the love of truth.

We can physically *train* someone to be brave, as sergeants drill
recruits by the brute repetition of running through exploding
fields, but this is not the learning of courage. There is no mere
exercise that can induce one to confront fear for the sake of goodness in itself. Indeed, very often the most spectacular kinds of
courage are precisely those that demand entirely unfamiliar
confrontations. It would seem, therefore, that the metaphor of
physical training is not at all isomorphic to the learning of moral
strength. Is Plato's analogy, then, misleading? It would indeed mislead if taken too literally. The analogy is not that, just as physical
training requires frequent repetition of instinctively repugnant
acts, so moral training requires actual confrontations with fear-

some challenges to our preferences. Rather it is the more simple notion that just as physical training teaches us to concentrate on the effort in spite of fearsome distractions, so moral education teaches us to focus on being good just for the sake of being good. The physical training of the soldier instills a reverence for the squad, platoon or regiment; moral education instills a reverence for the good as such. We cannot train anyone to be courageous merely by practicing dangerous maneuvers, but we can educate someone to concentrate on what it means to be good rather than to be satisfied. In moral strengthening we learn to focus on a different way of thinking: that who *we* are is more important that what I instinctively desire. The analogy with physical training is therefore valid only in these two ways: the intensification of concentration, and the shift from caring about private success to caring about the nobility of the confrontation. Courage is therefore sacrificial concentration on, and for the sake of, that which ennobles because of our belonging.

By these reflections we avoid accounting for moral strength in terms of some mysterious, metaphysical or causal agency, like the Will; and we also avoid spotting it as a mere psychological means for adhering to the moral law.

This emphasis upon the sequestration of courage from its role as a means to morality, however, though of fundamental importance, can be dangerously oversimplified. The worth of courage may be independent of its service to morality, but being moral and being virtuous are not antithetical; indeed they are interrelated without being interdependent. It is akin to confederation rather than federation, where the varying states retain their independence and sovereignty, yet still are capable of an intimacy that is not mere coexistence or even alliance, but a belonging-together that affords a common front.

A man lustful of an unwilling woman may risk considerable danger, pain and uncertainty when he embarks on the crime of rape, but we do not consider this confrontation of his fears as courage. But why not? It may take considerable boldness and daring to overcome very genuine fears, the lack of which may well indict him of unsavory meekness. Indeed, he may require more struggle with his own timidity than the courageous warrior who stands by his post during an attack. Yet, in spite of this boldness, there is con-

siderable reluctance to designate the rapist as courageous, if for no
other reason than that courage as a virtue cannot be wedded to a
vicious character. Does this mute the very sequestration between
virtue and morality that is laid out in Chapter 7 and is presumed
in the previous paragraphs? Morality deals with human actions; it
is possible to be good and do what is immoral just because action
and character are different. But in designating the rapist as a
wicked *character,* it becomes impossible to say a good man (i.e., a
good character) can be a bad man (i.e., a bad character). We
thereby avoid the stigma of logical contradiction; though in doing
so we have undoubtedly muddied what we might prefer to be
clearer. There is no doubt that the rapist is considered a wicked
character because, *in part,* his actions are immoral, and hence virtue and morality must be interrelated, though not interdependent.
But were the rapist to be indicted as wicked solely on the basis of
his immoral action, we could not allow the independence of virtue
from morality.

We thus do not want to say that moral strength is good only if it
succeeds in bringing about morally proper action, but we do want
to say that the agent must have personal integrity (as a self-judg-
ing judge) as well as a reverence for what is greater than oneself
that prompts the sacrificial confrontation of one's fears. The rapist
may have to confront his fears bravely, but since neither the integrity of judgment nor the sacrificial reverence inherent in courageous confrontation is present, he is judged not merely as one who
does an immoral act (for good men can do immoral acts) but as
being a wicked person or as having a wicked character.

The moral law, after all, dictates our actions; it does not constitute our ethical character. Because it is an *absolute* command, it
cannot be seen as a mere means by which we achieve the status of
being good. I do not revere what are mere means or maps. Thus
the moral law is what it is not only because it tells us what to do,
but also because, its origin being greater than our personal existence, inspires reverence. But by itself, even if it is followed with all
due obedience, it cannot qualify the adherent as a good man. Without moral strength it may be psychologically impossible for me to
adhere to the moral law, but it does not follow that moral strength
has worth and meaning only when conjoined to such adherence;
nor does it follow that the moral law is merely a chart by which we

guide the virtues. The moral law is not merely obeyed, it is revered, and it is revered in part not only because it guides our action but also because of its origin.

But these reflections seem to have darkened rather than brightened the landscape. First we insist that virtue and morality be entirely distinct; but now we insist they also must interrelate, without being interdependent. Mere metaphors, such as the political distinctions between confederation and union, may help, but they do not satisfy. We question not what it means to be moral or even what it means to be virtuous, but more fundamentally, what it means to be good. Virtue and morality are subsets of being good; neither by itself suffices; perhaps not even both together suffice. Both may be necessary, but neither singly or together are sufficient. It is for this reason that the question is formulated in terms of what it means to be good. The focus is thus on the *meaning* of being good, that is, on how we think about being good. Just as we think about what it means to be bad in terms of a weakness that yields to temptation, so we think about what it means to be good in terms of the moral strengthening that sacrificially concentrates on that which ennobles us by participating in what is greater than our personal existence. The philosophical error would be to assume that it were more fundamental to discover causes, faculties, or psychological conditions to account for this strengthening. This would be an error because meaning always precedes the agency or machinery by which the meaning is accomplished. The labor outranks the tools, the journey outranks the carriage. What it means to be good outranks the conditions that make it possible.

Moral strengthening, therefore, is now revealed as the fundamental, nonreducible second way of being good. It might seem that the inquiry should now directly turn to the third way of being good; but it is first necessary to introduce a transition. In order to show the necessity of the third way, a brief interlude will be considered in which we ask what is the most vexing and troubling kind of moral and ethical dilemma that we can confront.

10

The Most Troubling Moral Judgment (Transition)

In seeking to understand what it means to be a mountain climber, it is important to ask which of all the peaks is the most difficult to ascend. We ask this not to challenge the bold but to learn the fullest extent of confronting such majestic heights. In reflecting on the most troubling climb, we realize why this particular ascent is the most formidable, and thereby learn about what it means to climb at all. Or, in speculating on what is the thorniest case for a jurist, we can appreciate the complex but dreadful magnificence of the law. Such questions are not idle parlor games. To understand the greatest challenge in any endeavor is a way of learning about it, and to be able to discern the greatest challenge within any given enterprise may well require a highly developed familiarity with, or even mastery of, the subject. Accordingly, it is of capital significance to ask: What is the most troubling moral judgment we can confront?

The question does not ask which moral decisions are the most painful or which have the direst consequences. Rather, to pose this question is deliberately to press the limits of our moral deliberations, putting our understanding of what it means to be good in a crucible, as it were, to test the soundness and the mettle of our judgment. For only when our understanding of what it means to be good is vexed in the extreme can we lay claim to the thoroughness that marks a genuine philosophical inquiry. Consequently, this question not only deserves our attention, it becomes a pivotal step in the development of this study.

To what extent, if any, is it permitted a morally good person to intrude into another's willful, immoral behavior? Are we not required to take every step available to stop evil from happening? Yet, are we not also required, by dint of our respect for the integrity of others, to let them be the masters of their own moral destiny? Lest the acuteness of this dilemma be muted by distraction, it should be clarified that we are not concerned with questions in which third and innocent parties may also lay claim to our assistance. It seems clear that, were a child about to be molested, I not only have the right but the duty to intervene. But the justification for such intrusion is the right of this victim to expect assistance. It is not obvious, however, that I have the right to stop another mature and competent person from corrupting himself, degrading himself, violating trusts, lying, or breaking promises. It is not even clear that I always have the right to keep another from hurting a third party. Do I have a right or duty to stop a woman from cheating on her husband? Quite simply the question is this: In order to be good, must I allow another to be bad? Or must I always try to stop another from doing wrong?

The question has its parallel on the political level. During the agonizing period prior to the election of Abraham Lincoln, our nation was forced to confront this issue with all of its huge and troubling import. Stephen Douglas insisted that, though he despised slavery, he could not justify the people of the sovereign state of Illinois telling the people of the sovereign state of South Carolina how they must live their lives. Even today these agonizing questions haunt us. By what right can one country force another to act decently? We hesitate to send troops onto foreign soil even if acts of barbarous injustice are being perpetrated there. This hesitation is not always due to political delicacy or military impotence; there is a very real reluctance to violate sovereignty simply because of what sovereignty means. If sovereignty is to nations as integrity is to individuals it would seem this same reluctance must impede our intrusion into private outrages.

Is the matter as simple as Douglas assumes? Given the sovereignty of states or the integrity of individuals, are we rendered entirely impotent in stopping another from wrongdoing? But if, in any sense at all, I am my brother's keeper, if we are a human family and share the guilts and triumphs with others, it may seem imperative that the one social obligation that stands out above all others is this one: that I must frustrate the wrongs my fellows would otherwise commit. And, since we have shown that virtue is always a kind of learning, can we stand idly by as our children associate with dangerous characters and do nothing? Is not one of the greatest indictments of our age that we seem more indifferent to the pollution of our cultural atmosphere than to the meteorological? Do we stand back and let the haters of our heritage unsweeten our music, unrhyme our poetry, undress our children, unravel our marriages, undignify our language, and unleash the jackals of gratification to snap and snarl at a carrion culture? To espouse noninvolvement in the wrongs of others is to become like Leibniz's monads, windowless; we become isolated, lonely, selfish units, unworthy of any common warmth or moral adhesion. We become the very islands that the adage assures us no man is.

We have dwelt within the turmoil of this question long enough to adopt our usual, prudential response: we compromise. To avoid the draconian extremes we balance this indictment of moral disinterest with the counterindictment of intrusionary meddling and seek a middle ground. We can talk, entreat, plead and even yell at our brother for taking drugs or hurting his wife by a wanton affair, but we do not expose his dealings to the narcotic squad nor exile the offending harlot from his reach. We say we can persuade, but not force, and thereby serve two masters. But this is the guile that deceives only ourselves. Yelling at our brother's wrongs comforts only our own unease, it does not improve or even comfort him. And if our yelling does indeed succeed, then have we not already intruded? To say we disapprove of impregnating children, but refrain from sufficient action to impede it is simply hypocrisy, for to disapprove *is* to frustrate, else approval and disapproval become only ashes in our mouths.

Yet, to frustrate the evil of others necessarily intrudes into that sacred realm of sovereignty without which there is no government, or integrity without which there is no morally significant person. Are we then bound to be either hypocrites or puritans? Are we compelled to let our world rot with corruption by noninvolvement, or intrude wantonly like tyrants and eclipse all freedom? It is precisely because there is no true middle ground, but only the prudential balance that is a self-deception perhaps more heinous than either extreme, that this is the most troubling of all moral judgments.

Not even God, apparently, can escape it. He could have figured out a way, being all-wise, to have derailed Satan's temptation of Eve. Why did he not? To say that Eve's freedom accounts for his noninvolvement condemns the whole world's long history to a malignant anguish. Is this good? And God, it seems, in a huge joke, created his advocate, John Milton, to explain this sanctity of integrity that lost us paradise, and made him a Puritan, entirely unreluctant to force by means of the sword a stern code of conduct on his fellow merry Englishmen.

This is the most vexing problem within the confines of what it means to be good because it reveals a conflict that, left only to the machinery of moral and ethical reasoning, cannot be resolved. It is entirely valid to insist that because South Carolina is corrupt in its support of slavery, it must be forced, by the use of arms if necessary, to desist in the evil practice. It is likewise entirely valid to argue that such intrusion into the sovereignty of a state is unwarranted, and cannot be justified. We justify intrusion on the grounds that only if the wicked are stopped can we achieve a virtuous existence; we justify nonintrusion on the grounds that, in order to be moral, we must be free even to do what is wicked. If the moral question is "What ought I to do?" and the ethical question is "How can I be good?," then, in this most troubling question, the limits of both ethics and morality are breached. They must conflict. Just as in the case of the earlier question whether a good man can do a bad thing, so this present reflection on the most troubling dilemma elaborates the distinction. But, in asking if a good man can do a bad thing the purpose of the analysis was to show that there is a real difference between the ethical and the moral. Here the purpose goes beyond the distinction to show that the conflict itself forces us to realize an entirely different methodological question.

The threat of moral misology requires that, confronted with this troubling dilemma we cannot simply abandon our rational inquiry altogether, and submit to relativism or irrationalism. The valid but conflicting authority of both of these important questions does not show that our philosophical resources are bereft of any response, but rather that our arsenal is not limited to these two important questions. There is another question within the battery of philosophical armament that reveals something important about our being good. We ask not only what we ought to do, which is a moral question in the narrow and precise sense, nor how to achieve goodness, which is an ethical question concerned with acquiring virtues, but we also ask what it means to be good, which is concerned with moral truth. The first question asks about the moral law, the second about the achievement of virtues, and the third asks about being good as a mode of our existence. It is necessary for the first two questions to conflict in order for the third to be *asked.*

It is only in the torturous vexation of the most troubling dilemma that we are compelled to shift our probing from questions that are responded to by terminating resolutions to a question that, when confronted, does not resolve but illuminates. It is not the action, or the virtuous life, but the meaning of being good that is revealed.

This enforced discovery of the third path does not invalidate or even "transcend" either the moral or the ethical. Rather, the third method of confronting goodness is possible only because the moral law is absolute and the achievement of the virtues is necessary. But to do what we ought to do and to live a good life are not sufficient. We do not merely act, nor do we merely live virtuously, nor do we merely conjoin these, and do both. We also *reflect.* And what we reflect upon is meaning. Therefore, how we reflect, either wisely or foolishly, also becomes an essential mark of being good. The appeal to this third question cannot *resolve* the anguish or the risk of this or any moral or ethical dilemma, for then it would not be distinct from the simply adherence to the moral law.

We must, of course, act; and a realization of the limits of moral and ethical reasoning of itself cannot determine how we ought to act. But this reflective or third discovery can illuminate, that is, show us what it means to be good or bad. The passion for mere activist resolution is here dangerous to truth. This is part of what it means to speak of the risk of being.

It is perhaps now clear why the above-mentioned appeal to prudential compromise may be indicted as possibly more heinous than puritanical intrusion or hypocritical noninvolvement. What is repulsive is not that we act in a compromising way, but that such resolution be seen as the solution to a moral and ethical puzzle. This is no puzzle that can be solved, as if one need only fit the pieces of ethical goodness to interlock with moral obligation. It is rather a fundamental and profound risk, that is weighed not in terms of its success, and even less in terms of fortuitous consequence, but of the denuding power of its truth. It is the final weapon in the arsenal of being good: It shows us who we are.

But who are we, then? What does this conflict tell us about our being bad or good? To watch a friend yield to the swirling forces of a vortex that will drag him into the current of disaster cannot be borne without involvement, else I forfeit the honored title of friend. To eclipse a friend's autonomy by such forceful involvement that it is I, not he, who overcomes, is to deny him his greatest boon, the right, if not to triumph, at least to learn by his failure. To intrude at all, even by the gentlest warning, is to encroach upon his autonomy; to set limits to my influence, however distant, is to abandon him when most he needs my succor. The compromise, permitting ourselves limited intervention, may seem the only practical solution, but it begs the question, for either I succeed in influencing or I do not; if so, I have intruded, if not I have abandoned.

What the reflection affords is a new way of thinking about what it means to be good. It is to be at risk. It is to expose the supreme intimacy of our souls, that precious, private, and secret vulnerability that is our core of strength. It is that very origin of good and bad that is not dictated by anything else, but that, when exposed, shows us who we are. It is, as it is shown. It is not some thing, some faculty, or hidden quality that can be isolated and set apart. It is rather a way of being.

A crow, to eat and dig for worms, needs a beak. To grasp its prey it needs a talon or a claw. To fly it needs wings. In these cases we say the function needs a faculty. But the crow in flight can soar, or glide, can dive or circle. Soaring, gliding, diving and circling do not need special faculties; they are simply ways of flying. There is no special feather to account for this activity or that. And so to be good or bad is not accounted for by special tools or agencies, but are ways of being. To be able to be good or bad requires only to be who we are, and to reflect upon who we are is one of the essential ways that make up who we are, as gliding, soaring, and diving "make up" flying.

To reflect on who we are is thus, along with judging and moral strength, the third way to be good that emerges when the first two conflict, and hence show themselves as incomplete. But this reflection, in which who we are is denuded and hence exposed, has a unique meaning not revealed merely by moral strength and judgment.

The term "denuding" is crucial. To denude is to expose, to show what is hidden, and hence it is akin to being truthful or making truth happen. This suggests that being good is not only something we become, or something we do, but something that is meaningful in its truth. There is a connection, in other words, between truth and goodness, just as Plato suggests.

But denuding also carries a powerfully negative connotation. It is a usurpation or invasion of privacy and sacredness; it intrudes into what does not belong to the public world. There is inherent in the word, a sense of being stripped naked before leering or contemptuous eyes, of being made shameful by forced revelation of what is secret and precious. How can such violation of our innermost treasure ever be a part of goodness? If truth means exposure, need it always be good? And what is it that is exposed?

The third way of being good is character. Does this transitional chapter imply then, that what is exposed or revealed in the truth of goodness is nothing other than character? The most vexing judgment thereby also becomes the most denuding judgment. To intrude into another's integrity may well be morally justified, but such intrusion is also a denuding of the intruder. To enter into this stygian arena is to undergo a kind of enforced nakedness that exposes our vulnerability. We cannot be good, it seems, without being vulnerable. There is a paradox here, but its illumination is beyond the limits of a mere transitional question. But in turning to the issue of character, we are now prepared to undress it with an eye toward its alluring though retreating vulnerability. For it is our character that is denuded; it is our character that is vulnerable; it is our character that shows us, perhaps exotically, that the truth of goodness matters absolutely.

11

The Third Way of Being Good: Character

After entreating the hapless Guildenstern to play the pipe on which he possesses no skill, Hamlet upbraids him with this keen-edged analogy:

> Why, look you now, how unworthy a thing you make of me!
> You would play upon me; You would seem to know my stops;
> you would pluck out the heart of my mystery; you would
> sound me from my lowest note to the top of my compass:
> and there is much music, excellent voice, in this little organ;
> yet cannot you make it speak? S'blood, do you think that I
> am easier to be played on than a pipe?

The outraged censure here speaks not merely to the inept malice of the treacherous Guildenstern, but to all and any who seek to "pluck out the heart of our mystery" as if our fundamental character were available to human mastery by the mere learning of a skill. The protest is not that this particular wretch is inept, but that anyone at all would think the very heart of our mystery can be so reduced. For, indeed, if it be a mystery, any attempt to anatomize it, label it, classify it, and hence play upon it is fruitless and rests on bad thinking. This warning from the tragic prince must be taken seriously. The heart of our mystery is precious to us, and all who would seek to pluck it out are left with the shameful sobriquet of a philosophic Guildenstern.

But it is the very mystery of what is precious that renders it elusive to our philosophical probing. For if we must, as seekers, penetrate into our own inner darkness, how then can we retain our secrets? To keep ourselves unpillaged by the marauders of analysis we apparently must take refuge in a coyness unbefitting philosophy. Like a troubled state questioning the right of the individual to privacy but also caring about the right of the public to know and the ubiquitous press to peer, we seem to be involved in a paradox that threatens to eclipse the very sun we seek. How can we ask about character if the essence of character is to keep itself secret? We fail as philosophers if we abandon the search, but we fail as character if we let the search succeed.

Were we to pluck out the heart of our mystery by reducing who we are to principles, elements, and causes beyond ourselves, we would not only violate the precious, we would also fail as philosophers. For we need not ask what the secret is, as if by knowing it, all secretion is erased, but rather we can ask what it means to be secreted at all. If the third way of being good is to keep intact one's inner, irreducible character, what it means to hold oneself as precious can be examined without having to disregard our mystery. For we can surely ask what it means to keep a secret without revealing what the secret is. Such a response will not satisfy the reductionist, but to reduce is not to understand but to make palatable to already existing tastes. We do not seek to account for character by reducing it to something else, for the whole point of this inquiry is to discover the three separate and hence nonreducible ways to be good.

Nevertheless, there is a challenge to traditional principles in raising this question solely it terms of what it means to hold something as precious and not to focus on what kind of thing is being held. How is it possible even to raise such a question, much less to answer it? An analogy may be helpful.

Not all intimacy is sexual; indeed, the carnal may be relatively insignificant in comparison to other forms of intimacy. Nevertheless, the language of the sexual may serve as a model just because of its universal and persuasive familiarity. Accordingly, we can watch the revealing development of a pubescent teen as he first encounters these dimensions in himself. He does not originally discover that his body is first private, and then, because it is precious in its privacy, want to share it only with his first beloved. Rather, it is the other way around. It is *first* in his intimate sharing that he is aware of its preciousness. Having denuded himself to her, his privacy *becomes* precious. Prior to this, mere convention kept him covered, in an enforced modesty that both curiosity and boyish playfulness may often violate. At this coltish stage he does not mind his saucy fellows playing on him like a pipe, for there is, as yet, no reason for keeping secret what is not yet precious. Indeed, being without secrets of this kind may well constitute that unrecoverable innocence when friendships are iron bands, a day in summer has no sunset, and hope is unnecessary. There really can be no nakedness among children. But once denuded, in a maturing that makes the uncovering *precious*, the idle, merry exposures of the boy are no longer possible. Now he wants to be covered, not out of shame but out of esteem for his own dignity. He would uncover only for her, which makes it precious. He may know that all men, in this regard, are alike; that what he covers is as common as any other part of him that is shared by all members of his gender. But, such knowledge is not what matters. Because he shared it with her, it is not common at all. Thus the intimacy that denudes makes possible the preciousness, which is private. The exposure makes it secret.

The seeming paradox of these five words is part of our mystery. When this simple analogy to venereal education is applied beyond the image, however, the truth of it is powerful. We now must read these five words in an entirely nonsexual way. We understand "precious" now to mean that which is dear and important because of its privacy, because it belongs to us or we belong to it. The denuding does not destroy this preciousness, but rather makes it possible.

Guildenstern's insulting behavior is offensive because in his treatment of Hamlet as a puzzle to be solved, he forfeits what is precious. Yet, in his protest against this vulgar treatment, Hamlet denudes, that is, exposes, the sequestering of what is his own. By showing to us that the heart of his mystery matters, he has exposed what it means to be precious. The ensuing exposure is an uncovering always *as* precious, hence as sequestered.

At this point to insist that we ask what is secret and exposed is to miss the point entirely. For the answer, "We are the exposed secret," is both too obvious and too subtle. It tells us nothing just because it tells us everything. What matters is not that we are what is secreted, but that being exposed secretly is a distinct and separate way to be good.

It is not enough simply to be who we are; we must also reflect on who we are if we are to be good in this third way. This reflection provides a kind of "knowledge" of oneself, but it is knowledge in a rather special sense, perhaps more adequately expressed by the term "intimacy."

It is the epistemology of this kind of self-denuding intimacy or reflection that is crucial. In order to reflect, one must somehow be disjoined into knower and known, and this in turn is possible only because of a reflector. I can reflect only by being a reflector of myself as reflected. Just as in the physical realm I can see myself only by means of a mirror, so to succeed as character I must reflect upon or "mirror" who I am. This means not only having a heart of my mystery, but also being able to reflect upon it; and so, the image of myself must be pulled back or away from myself in order to see it. The preciousness is violated by the denuding, but only because of the violating—which in this case is the stepping back from—can the precious exist at all. It is precious because it is denuded.

What bestows the very preciousness that makes it worthwhile is its being denuded, in which what is denuded is its very privacy and sequestration. Hamlet insists upon the heart of his mystery just as the maturing but youthful lover insists upon covering what is precious as private. But neither Hamlet's mystery nor the youth's privacy can matter until and unless it is revealed (or denuded) by a reflective intimacy.

To respect truth as inherent in one's being reflected is a way to be good; and to be able to be reflected upon as privately precious is what we mean by character. In other words, it is not merely that we are reflected in our own denuding, but that the reflecting is true, that "characterizes" us—that is, makes who we are matter. Such reflecting is meaningless unless it reveals to us who we are in truth.

It may be entirely noncontroversial that unless we each have a certain sense of "being special," a sense of ultimate uniqueness that we hold protectively close and treasure dearly, we have no claim to character. What is less clear is that the truly precious is not what is held dear but the holding dear itself. For, to be able to treasure and protect what is our own is what makes it dear in the first place. Corruption, which is becoming bad as character is countered by a kind of nobility that is becoming good as character. Corruption consists precisely in not being able to treasure what is dear, letting the heart of our mystery be plucked out by some wanton Guildenstern.

The etymology of the term has led some to think our character is imprinted on us by early training or the factors of inheritance. But it is the active and not the passive voice that determines here. It is not we who are imprinted with this stamp but we who imprint or make our mark. And it is not the form or signet itself, but our stamping it on our behavior that is character. The results of being imprinted by nurture and nature is our personality; our character lies in being able to keep intact the precious meaning of who we are. The extent to which this meaning is reflected in our character is the extent to which we become a mirror. But this mirror, if our character is to achieve the lofty status of nobility, cannot merely be for us as individuals, it must also mirror our belonging. Art works are mirrors in this sense: we see in them reflections of our humanity that we cannot see in any other way, as a concrete universal. This is why it is philosophically sound to reflect upon our great cultural sacraments as a way of revealing truth. But if we are able to reflect our cultural reality the way an art work does, we become ourselves a kind of reflective model of our cultural reality, which is to be noble. The noble are not only within a culture, they also reflect it; and if their reflection achieves a degree of universality in its uncovering, they become like works of art. In this way the nobility of Lincoln reflects the universal truth of what it means to be an American, Mother Teresa reflects what it means to be a Christian, Robert E. Lee reflects what it means to be a warrior. These three are not artists, nor are they strictly speaking, art works; but their stories function as art works do. All of us, except for the totally corrupt, have character, but only a few achieve nobility of character to the extent of being mirrors of our cultural reality. Nevertheless, however minute it may be, the germ of that possibility, of having such radiance as to reflect the universal meaning of who we are, constitutes our character. And it is because of this potentiality for nobility, that our character is a way of being good. Because we are also capable of becoming corrupt, our character is also a way of being bad.

There is a mild paradox in the claim that being good as character is both a retention of what is precious and at the same time a paradigm or mirror of the universal, for it may seem as if the more distinctive and private we become the less available we are for universal mirroring. But this paradox is no more troubling than that it is always the rarely great who reflect universally. Mother Teresa's sanctity may be rare, but it still serves to illuminate what it means to be Christian, just as the talents and genius of Robert E. Lee are highly unusual, yet he serves as a model for all warriors. The ideal, in order to reflect the universal, cannot be common, any more than excellence can be ubiquitous. This is important, for goodness usually seems to require a selfless or even self-sacrificing quality that may not immediately appear consistent with the notion of keeping one's personal integrity intact.

Character is not some faculty or quality other than this: it is simply our being able to be noble or corrupt. Thus similes such as character being like soft wax or a blank slate on which the impressions of nobility or corruption are made are entirely misleading. There is no wax, there is merely being noble or corrupt. What is important is that this particular way of being good or bad is neither accountable by nor reducible to either judgment or moral strength. Hence, it is an irreducible and separate way to be good.

But even colloquial thinking admits that we cannot give of ourselves unless there first be something in us that is worth giving, even as we also admit that it may be only in giving of ourselves that we develop anything within us that is worth while. Bad character not only corrupts who we are, it also fouls the social environment; good character not only ennobles what is precious, it also brightens the moral landscape. It is how we think about character: not merely as private preserve but as shared belonging. But these are not two, distinct qualities of character, as if to share and to retain were different activities done at different times; they must be seen as fundamentally the same, the way the boy's privacy is precious only as shared.

Corruption, as we have seen, erodes the self by the collapse of all resistance to temptation; but in so doing it also becomes a contagion for others, not merely incidentally, but as a part of what it means to be corrupt. In the same way, nobility not only protects the self, it also radiates its dignity so as to dignify others. Character is nothing else except being able to be noble or corrupt, and hence character cannot be thought without the intimacy within our belonging.

It may seem almost inadvertent, therefore, that to be good is to measure oneself in universal terms. In light of the huge importance and centrality given to universalizing by Immanuel Kant it may seem that this account has slighted such an important aspect of our moral thinking. Kant, after all, insists that universality is the very essence of making moral claims, whereas these present reflections locate it as a dimension of character. But Kant seeks to establish the basis of the moral law; these reflections are rather concerned with meanings. It is in no way trivializing to recognize the connection between the Kantian account of the moral law and the present existential account of the radiating quality of character; but we must keep the kinds of inquiry separate. If universality is indeed the essence of the moral law then it should be reflected in how we raise the question of what it means to be good. But the present reflection asks not for the legitimacy of the governing principle but what being good means. Since character, as a way of keeping ourselves intact and not reduced to external forces, radiates its own integrity as a reflecting of what it means to be who we are, it achieves a kind of public or universal significance from which others as well as ourselves can learn. Being good is therefore not an entirely private matter. Indeed, to be good as character is distinct and separate; it is a fundamental way of being good. By means of the radiating of our character, whether good as noble or bad as corrupt, we learn the existential meaning of universality. The universal is not merely found in the formal decision procedure of applying general laws, it is also a way of being, a modality of truth.

And that it is truth, and not merely our own beliefs, or the peculiar prejudices of one tradition rather than another, needs to be emphasized. Whatever truth is embodied in Christianity or America is reflected by the nobility of Mother Teresa or Abraham Lin-

coln. Without their cultures neither could be noble, but what nobility radiates is not a mere local value or opinion but truth itself.
The fundamental need to share what is our own by way of a culture is not an indicator of social relativism, but on the contrary, of
universal meaning. Different mirrors may reflect the same light in
different ways, but that the light is independent of one mirror or
the other is essential for the reflecting to occur. Human finitude
prevents direct access to the universal light, but human nature,
struggling with these limits, universalizes through cultural mirrors
that reflect truth itself. There is nothing to prohibit some mirrors
reflecting better than others, but to demote any cultural reflection
to mere local prejudice is to abuse what matters most; it is to
abuse not only ourselves but the possibility of any truth whatsoever. To discover that to reflect this universal, though mirrored,
truth is a fundamental way to be good is thus of great significance.
For being good must now be seen as both a personal and a public
affair, as both intensely private and hence precious and necessarily universal, and hence noble. This existential universality is
not an abstraction; it is not achieved by conceptual focus upon
similar qualities, the way we notice similar traits in collies and
spaniels, and thus arrive at the concept of a dog. It is rather concretely universal, the way a unique and rare *Hamlet* speaks to
every man. Because it is concrete it can be a way of being good.

Part Four

Confronting the Good

12

The Pathos of Being Good

In raising the question what it means to be good it is not enough merely to describe and reflect on the three ways of being good: judgment, moral strength, and character. Being good is not only possessing the faculties or virtue by which we do good things but it is also to be directly *aware* of being good. And since the emerging canon of this inquiry seems to be that we are always good and bad, we must also consider what it means to be directly aware of our own being bad. In the colloquial this question might be raised in terms of what it is *like* to be good or bad; perhaps we might even ask in nonphilosophical argot what it feels like to be good or bad.

But with the emergence of the term "feel" we enter into most unfriendly territory, since feelings are notoriously unstable and subjective, and apparently entirely unfitting for philosophical discourse. I may feel outraged at another's conduct that is quite undeserving of any censure. I may weep over what is in fact good fortune. My left hand may feel the warm water as cold at the same time my right hand feels the same water as hot. Thus, feelings are not only subjective but they can even be contradictory. These demerits have not dissuaded many thinkers from relying on feelings for, after all, the hedonist is entirely unashamed of placing the purely subjective feelings of pleasure on the master's throne of all ethics. But he does so in happy abandon of any universality or objectivity, which is unacceptable to the present inquiry.

Feelings are indeed woeful instruments of cognition; they fail wantonly as providers of knowledge of what is the case, for they not only differ from person to person, their very intensity often dulls the powers of discrimination and measured judgment. But this is simply to put a false burden on the wrong carriage. We do not ask for feelings to tell us about the way things are in the environment, but to reveal truths about ourselves. I may indeed be in shameful error in my outrage at a benefactor trying to do me well, but as we have seen in the analysis of *Julius Caesar*, this in no way impedes the philosopher from finding great truth in asking what outrage means. The passions, emotions and feelings may easily be distorted or misdirected, but as human phenomena they are disregarded at foolish peril. A kind of pathoempiricism is surely possible in which truth can be learned, and from which lessons can be discovered, that equal or even surpass sensed experience of external events. David Hume did not hesitate to designate these direct moral sentiments as "impressions," which were, to him, always superior to the less lively and less vivid ideas. There is thus both formal and historical support for raising the question concerning how we confront (and "feel") what it means to be good or bad.

Consistent with the tone and method, it is fitting to begin by asking what feeling, passion, or emotion reveals to us the experience of being bad. What, in other words, is the pathos of the bad? There are two answers, depending on whether being bad entirely dominates our character, or whether our wrongdoing is philosophically interesting and occurs in the broader context of being both good and bad. For the thoroughly wicked it seems the passion or feeling of being bad is a kind of manic glee in triumph over victims; approaching, though not quite achieving, the sadism in which the pleasure consists precisely in the inflicting of undeserved suffering on another. We do not wish to equate this delight in triumphing by illegitimate and even cruel means with true sadism, for this would render what is analyzed into a species of mental aberration. We are not speaking of the perverse but of the wicked, and surely the revealing pathos of being bad for the entirely corrupt is delight taken in cruel triumph. Nietzsche describes this elation in sheer animal conquest, indifferent to the suffering of the victim or even the dubiety of the devious means taken to achieve it, as a characteristic of the blond beast who sees only the bad—identified as unfitting the noble—and never the evil, which is a force greater and other than the noble ones. Misguided reading of Nietzsche may mislead us to the belief that Nietzsche approves of this satisfaction taken in conquering others, but such shallow reading of a great thinker need not distract us beyond the simple need to fleck the offending insect off the page. What it means to be bad for the wicked, then, must obviously take the form of somehow embracing or, at the very least, submitting to, the very status of badness itself. It is, in a way, a rather juvenile glee in that false superiority over the staid, the proper, and the repressed urgency of natural wants that so attracts the indifferentist seeking both distraction and a curious self-esteem based upon the contempt of the disciplined. We feel good just because we feel wicked.

But these are fairly extreme types, and are of little philosophical interest precisely because they are one-dimensional. Far more frequent and far more interesting are those who indeed share the glee in their alienation from the bovine good, but who also wince at the sting and burden of guilt. The pathos of the ordinary bad is thus a kind of tension created by the lure for mischievous glee and the shame or regret that roils our conscience. Those who are entirely overcome only by the guilt are even rarer than the thoroughly wicked and are as perverse as the sadist. Indeed it is tempting to speculate that the absolutely guilty are disingenuous and self-deceitful, flagellating themselves with the whips of guilt either as a rabid and self-induced punishment so as to avoid true censure, or even as a species of masochistic delight in which the pleasure is taken solely because one is so spectacularly guilty that one achieves an importance unavailable by any other trick. So it is neither the one burdened by guilt to the level of dysfunctional self-abasement nor the one who takes unmitigated and unholy glee in wrongdoing for its own sake that matters. To ask what it is like to be bad—which is admittedly a colloquial and hence imprecise locution—is to focus on the gleeful guilty: the one who is burdened by authentic guilt and yet is also delighted in the success of his guilty cunning. Nowhere is this more radiantly revealed than in Claudius's plea:

> But, O, what form of prayer
> Can serve my turn? Forgive me my foul murder!—
> That cannot be; since I am still possess'd
> Of those effects for which I did the murder—
> My crown, my own ambition, and my queen.
> May one be pardoned and retain the offence?

Claudius suffers true guilt, but retains the delights of doing wrong. In this he represents the true and universal confrontation of being bad; it is, to make an uncertain though believable empirical claim, what most of us "feel" when we reflect on our own badness. There is a burden of indebtedness upon us that seems to darken all we do. But there is also a peculiar singularity about it that specifies; we become uniquely ourselves only when guilt fingers us as the one to be singled out.

We have learned from the analysis of temptation that to be truly seduced requires both allure and resistance. The guilty, as Claudius realizes, can neither forfeit the lust that drove him to sin nor forget in the delight of that sin the burden that points him out. To be aware of this double-hooked lure is to confront what it means to be bad. We take delight in the usufructs of our crime even as we seek out darkened alleys to hide from the shameful glare of guilt. What is so important about this analysis is that it reflects the true meaning of good and bad as reciprocal notions: except in the rarest of cases we are neither perfectly good nor totally bad; and hence properly to understand either is to see them as contenders for hegemony within a soul struggling with itself. What we learn about being bad must therefore also provide us with at least structural insights into being good. If the pathos of being bad is guilt and glee, what then is the pathos of being good, illumined by these discoveries?

There are three obvious contenders. The first is pleasure; for who would deny that pleasure is good? A life entirely bereft of any and all pleasure strikes us as so unattractive, indeed so repugnant, that we cannot accept such an existence as good. Pleasure is more than mere gratification of base wants; it can be refined and even noble. We understand gratification as a negative: because I am hungry, I eat. Eating therefore negates the pain of hunger. But suppose I eat not to rid myself of the pain of hunger but simply to

please my palate. I eat because it tastes good, not because I am
hungry, and such eating—which perhaps should be called "din-
ing"—is not negative but positive: it is sheer pleasure. Indeed, this
is the true glory of pleasure, that it is not necessary; the greatest
pleasures are those that are gratuitous. It is precisely because
there is no compulsion or obligation to smell a rose or watch a
sunset that gives pleasure its unique satisfaction. I do not have to
defend it either on the grounds of morality, health, or logical necessity. Pleasure pleases; that is its radiance and its wonder.

It is also why pleasure cannot be the pathos of being good. It is
oddly a burden to place upon the graceful, lovely shoulders of pleasure the heavy yoke of morality. Let us leave at least a shrinking
number of precious things like pleasure and beauty their own existential worth, not freighting them with the heavy tonnage of the
moral or the ethical. We thus do not disqualify pleasure on the
grounds that some pleasures are bad, for that would not suffice.
Rather it is disqualified on existential grounds: pleasure pleases
without justification of any sort, hence it is entirely disconnected
with moral goodness.

The second candidate is far more honored by philosophers: The
pathos of the good is happiness. To be good, they say, is to be
happy. But how are we to understand happiness as other or more
than pleasure? We have volumes to tell us this; a eudaemonian
ethics has been favored by dozens of major thinkers throughout
the millennia. Some, such as the utilitarians, even go so far as to
add arithmetic to being happy; though why it is better to love two
women moderately than one passionately escapes me, even though
I know that three is numerically greater than two. But whether by
arithmetical means, or more sophisticated analyses, it must be ad-
mitted that happiness is a mustang among moral concepts, wildly
riding unfettered across the plains, leaping over fences and avoiding corrals. It is an elusive concept just because its reference is a
state or disposition, not a passion like pleasure nor an adherence
to rule like duty. Happiness cannot be the pathos of goodness simply because it is not a pathos at all. The moment we try to explain
happiness as a feeling it seems no different than pleasure. To expand happiness beyond that, which is what every eudaemonian
does, is to unleash the mustang beyond the corral, and it is no
longer the immediately felt confrontation that is necessary for a

pathos. It is a rare sight to see a utilitarian truly happy as he grimly count the units of utility. And so pleasure fails because, though it certainly qualifies as a pathos, it cannot bear the burden of the moral without destroying its essence as unnecessary and unrequired. Happiness may be strong enough to bear the weight of the moral, but in doing so it stretches too far from the realm of feeling and concrete immediacy to be the pathos of the good. I may not know whether I am truly happy, but I always know when I am pleased.

The first two suggestions have proved wanting. Is there a third? We recall that the pathos of the bad was guilt coupled with distracting glee. The guilt burdens us as well as singles us out in shameful isolation; but the glee adheres to us like unsavory glue, preventing us from escaping the sticky burden that we desire even as we hide from the denuding glare that accompanies it. Perhaps from these negatives we can suggest a positive.

A burden is that which presses down; it makes us feel diminished and small. So its opposite should lift us up, and in so doing make us feel extended beyond our ordinary limits like an inflated balloon. The guilt puts us in a spotlight of shame from which we would escape into darkness; the opposite does not isolate but welcomes, and the light does not embarrass but glows with radiation. Guilt individualizes, its opposite universalizes, but with a magnifying of the self. Guilt is earned; the other is bestowed. The glee we take in wickedness is contemptuous; in the opposite the delight is gratefully accepted. The pathos of the good is therefore an uplifting, radiant welcome in which we gratefully accept the generous bestowal of a delight that is ecstatic. This is what we call joy.

Joy is the pathos of the good; it is the Humean "impression" of being good; the direct, experiential confrontation of what it is like to be good. Yet this cannot mean that all who are good are actually joyous. We may well consider a martyr, enduring dreadful suffering for the sake of his religion, as a good man; or a father enduring years of crushing, humiliating labor for the sake of his daughter as a saintly person. Indeed, the necessarily sacrificial element in goodness would seem to disqualify joy as the pathos of the good. But such examples rely too heavily upon the mere conditions that surround the subject. It was earlier noted that pleasure was not disqualified merely because some pleasures are bad. To say that joy is the pathos of the good is not to say that the good are always in a state of ecstasy. The question here is this: what is it that gives the martyr and the father the strength to endure these grim and crushing miseries for the sake of their beloveds? Is it not the possibility, or memory, or hope, of joy? But when speaking of the pathos of the good these examples show something even more impressive. The passion and the love of the father for his daughter and the martyr for his faith are both intense and joyous feelings even though they occasion pain and suffering. To say that joy is the pathos of the good does not entail that the conditions are always present to make the good joyous, for then it would be the conditions and not the good itself that would make us joyous. It is rather to say that joy, as the pathos of the good, tells us what being good means. Perhaps only the good can be joyous. The false good of the wicked is called glee.

Joy reaches beyond ourselves; perhaps it even elevates us to a communion with greater powers. There is almost always a sense of gratitude that accompanies joy, as if we are bestowed with an ecstasy undeserved or at least unearned. This gratitude toward the transcending, bestowing power is not one of whimpering, pitiful thanks found in the destitute's reception of necessities, but a celebratory triumph of welcome and belonging. It is rather difficult to imagine the lonely or the friendless as joyful. For some, indeed, the truly joyous, as opposed to the gleeful, must be theistic in their ecstasy, so overwhelming is their experiential sense of belonging, gratitude, wonder and goodness.

But this listing seems somewhat unanchored. The search for a concrete phenomenon to analyze directs our need and attention to one of the most glorious paeans ever attributed to a human pathoempirical experience. It is precisely because Frederich Schiller's "Ode to Joy" is a source of truth that Ludwig van Beethoven added his magnificent music to make it an everlasting treasury from which the thinker can mine such extraordinary, truth-bearing ore. This conjoined masterpiece is recognized even by many who favor neither poetry nor classical music as being a true vehicle of its title: It is not only called the ode to joy, it also succeeds in bringing joy directly to the listener. But, more important, it is a cultural resource that deserves careful and penetrating analysis as a source of truth.

The opening line of Schiller's poem states the immediacy of the pathos with a remarkable poetic term *Götterfunken*—divine spark. Joy is the flint of God, a beautiful fire that flashes within us, directly reminding us that our passion for beauty and goodness is concretized as a direct-felt response to God's intrusion: *Freude schöner Götterfunken*—Joy, thou lovely spark of God. Joy itself is depicted as a daughter of Elysium—hence joy procedes from happiness, perhaps even surpassing it. But the image of joy as a kind of inward fire is repeated, for we approach the shrine of joy *feuertrunken*—drunk with fire. The two terms, *Götterfunken* and *feuertrunken*, reiterate the fundamental metaphor of fire in rhymed reinforcement.

Second only to the centrality of fire is the image of joy as a unifier—*Alle Menschen werden Brüder*—all men become brothers, under the wing of the goddess, Joy. A friend becomes a friend—*Eines Freundes Freund zu sein*—and a man who wins a noble woman—*ein holdes Weib*—are unified under the spell of the goddess. He who is joyless, however, must slink away, lonely and sorrowfully. The poem then begins to take on a slightly different caste and syntax: *Freude trinken alle Wesen / An den Brüsten der natur*—from the very breast of Nature drink all of joy's essence, suggesting again the universal creativity that this passion offers. But the following lines are even more astounding—*Alle Guten, alle Bösen / Folgen ihrer Rosenspur*—all the good and all the evil follow in her path. This cannot mean that joy embraces both the wicked and the good indifferently; rather it expresses one of the most central themes of this inquiry: joy, and indeed goodness itself, presupposes the fundamental nature of our reality as both good and bad; it is the realization that being itself is a cauldron of seething, fundamental, restless struggle between conflicting powers, good and evil, which are both concrete possibilities. The metaphysical wrestling to achieve order out of chaos—which is the mythical account of creation—reaches its most sublime moment in the triumph of union over discord, which is joy. This is not an erasure or forfeiture of bad, which must forever be a concrete possibility, but a mastering of it, the way a nuclear reactor controls the terrible fury of fission without muting its power; or to make a more classical comparison, the way the charioteer must firmly whip the dark horse into obedience without losing its love-strength in Plato's myth of the love-chariot in the *Phaedrus.* This, then is the risk of being—it is not our risk in taking up being, and certainly not a pious urge to take risks—it is *being's* risk in accepting the human as part of itself. This theme will be expanded in a later section.

In that part of the poem that Beethoven gives to the tenor solo, Schiller shifts his emphasis again, urging us to see joy, not as a mere delight subsequent to achievement, but as the quest itself of a knightly hero on his way to triumph—*Freudig wie ein Held zum Siegen.* In this passage we can find support for our distinction between glee and joy, which also awaits further analysis.

In the final stanza the poet brings home the most powerful truth learned in the confrontation of joy. First is the direct claim that all who are embraced by this passion must, or at least should, feel the inevitable presence of a Creator; that glee may be atheistic but joy cannot—*Ahnest du den Schöpfer, Welt?*—Do you feel the Creator, World? Yet this line is not a mere pious assertion of God's existence; it also locates the inner core of joy's essence: creation. Not only the creation of the world by God's power, but our own being creative, that is, being the *agent* of our own knightly triumphs within ourselves. Under the goddess, Joy, we become world-brothers, not in some naive utopia, but in the exhausted but elated realization that we, as free agents, matter; and that our joy is rooted in our realization that, beyond the stars—*Muss ein lieber Vater wohnen*—must a loving father dwell.

Schiller's poem makes joy concretely available as the pathos of the good. He is a truly great poet, perhaps the finest dramatic poet in the German language surpassing even Goethe. Yet, it is no disservice to Schiller to say that Beethoven's music lifts it to the level of the absolutely sublime. But the great musician does not merely put Schiller's poem to music, as one might write a melody for a song. Rather, his musical genius becomes a dramatic intensification of the themes and truths found not only in the poem but in the meaning of joy itself. It is the beginning of the kind of dramatic music that Wagner and Puccini would expand half a century, or even a whole century, later; music that establishes the mood and meaning of the various themes and passages, adding to them a profundity of understanding that only the symphonic or operatic could reveal. To understand joy as the pathos of the good, it is therefore enriching to examine how Beethoven does this. Since it is too much to expect the reader to have the score ready at hand, the language must remain general, and the references will be not to the score but to the text. But this will suffice, for the examination does not presume technical erudition; its goal is not musicology but philosophy.

The opening bars of the final movement of the Ninth Symphony prior to the singing, are troubled, harsh, discordant and busy. The tempo seems positively impatient, the earthy tones unsweetened with any loveliness. The great melodic and familiar theme is introduced without refinement, almost as if it is to be deemed a mere hurried passage; which, in a sense it is. For this transition from solid, almost angry power, made harsh by discord, to the chorale itself with all its sweet triumph is a lesson in joy; for joy is usually preceded by the harsh necessities of conflict, doubt, struggle and discord. It is not merely that such contrast makes the joyous more palpable by comparison, but that the sweetness of joy depends entirely on the troubling dissonance. There is no joy without precedent suffering.

The bass then begins to sing, in words written not by Schiller but Beethoven himself, telling us that the preceding furies are not the sounds we want. The very first word, *Freunde!*—friends—addressed to us the listeners, is deliberately homophonic with the term *Freude!*, joy. The connection between joy and friendship is thus firmly established.

After the bass completes the preface, he turns to Schiller's poem, singing the first stanza in a wondrous echo with the tenors, suggesting a carom between the low but deeply serious, and the youthful loftiness that the pathos itself manifests. The entire choir with full orchestral tutti then take up the powerful familiar theme; but on this first occasion there is little harmonizing or counterpoint; it is too bold and too satisfying. With the line, *Und der Cherub steht vor Gott!*—And the angel stands before God—the lofty, sopranic majesty fills us with a sense of sweetness, awe, and wonder. This is the sacred triumph of joy as both celebratory and reverential.

There is then a dramatic pause, which precedes the central stanza beginning "*Froh. . .*" (Joy). The orchestral passage here is profoundly revealing. There is first a series of clumsy grunts from the bassoons, suggesting a tyro or youth entering insecurely into the cathedral of sound that has just preceded. This clumsy, but elegant beginning goes through a series of steady but dramatic changes: the clumsy gives way, gently, to a cheerful youthful bounce, as if becoming more sure of itself. There is then a brief passage of military march, with tattoos on the snare drum establishing a sense of honor and spirit. But this is followed by music of almost oratorical reverence, shifting from drill field to basilica, until finally it reaches true awe and even respectful wonder. These stanzas are not in Schiller's poem, they are entirely contributed by the composer, showing us the actual genealogy of joy itself.

The brief passage, initiated by the tenor's bright and clarion *Froh* to the glorious *zum siegen* gives a brighter color to the solemnity, as if Beethoven were always unwilling to allow the solemn and awe—inspiring dimensions of joy to eclipse the brighter, coltish urgency of the hopeful. To reinforce this, he has the entire chorus and orchestra return to the first stanza in furious contrapunctual orchestration in fortissimo. This is the triumphant middle, an unleashed joy in the ecstasy of sublime sound. It seems almost as if no more could possibly be achieved.

But then the male choir, almost hesitantly, begins the passage *Seid umschlungen Millionen*—be embraced all you millions—returning us to more complex orchestration and harmonies until, with the whole choir now singing the final line of the poem, *Über Sternen muss er wohnen*—beyond the stars must he [the Creator] live—the music achieves an almost spooky, tremulous awe; it is a reverence so eerie and ethereal, so otherworldly in its utter sensuousness, that joy itself seems denuded in its truth. For to be joyous is boldly to intrude our corporeal reality into the welcoming but fearsome realm of the entirely spiritual. It seems metaphysically impossible, a violation of Cartesian dualism, a profanation of the sacred that is so sacrilegious it becomes, by the metanoia of artistic and pious greatness, supreme holiness. Joy transforms the sacrilege into the sacramental.

These stanzas cannot eclipse the more general treatment. Rarely has the interweaving of different themes, tempos, modes, and even keys been accomplished on such a magnificent, sensuous level—a stroke of genius that reinforces the unifying power of joy. We are all, both good and bad, made brothers not out of some social contract or political theory, but in the single passion, the dominating

pathos of goodness itself, joy. The art no longer represents the object, but brings it about; it is not merely joyful music but musical
joy. It is also, as we have seen in the analysis of the stanza beginning with the word *Froh,* a paean of hope. But this is not a hope for
a better world, but a world made better by hope. It is the pathos,
the feeling, of being good. And its truth is a gift from Beethoven's
genius.

The distinction between glee and joy, though sound, and essential for this analysis, is nevertheless dangerous, for it tempts the
thinker to list his private preferences under the latter and his private dislikes under the former, just because the distinction itself is
so promising. Thus, because I prefer Margaux to Beaujolais, I de-
clare the taste of the first to be joyous, the second to be merely
gleeful, and that to the unsophisticated. Any distinction of this sort
suffers the abuse of the shallow, but such misappropriation need
not forfeit entirely the legitimacy of the distinction. We may certainly comprehend that joy and glee are distinct phenomena without being assured of every item or member in each category. The
distinction is not made to fill up each class with all its possible
members, as if this were a taxonomic study. We make the distinction because taking delight in being bad is different from taking
delight in being good. As descriptions of feelings, the reader must
accept or reject the distinction on the basis of what he himself can
experience, though a personal, private rejection no more invali-
dates the distinction than a private acceptance confirms it. But
those of broad experience and sensitivity to language realize the
need for such a distinction, and the terms "glee" and "joy," taken
cautiously and provisionally, can be beneficial to such an inquiry.

There may be few who would doubt that the conjunction of Schiller's poetry and Beethoven's music does indeed tell us much about
joy itself. Perhaps it even succeeds in showing that joy is the pathos of the good. But even if we provisionally accept this, what
have these reflections provided for our understanding of the central theme: what does it mean to be good? Two notions, both of
which had been hinted at in earlier discussions, now become more
openly available. The first is the satisfying realization that goodness need not be restricted to abstract concepts or the performing
of good acts. What I have called the "pathos" of the good reveals
that the thematic question of what it means to be good has a pa-

thoempirical basis, that is: an experiential foundation that can be criticized and analyzed. The second advantage is even greater, though far more knotty; and this is the notion inherent in the title that what it means to be good is a risk to our being. To be good is possible, and to be bad is possible. Hence our own existence is fundamentally grounded in these opposing possibilities. We cannot escape it: goodness and badness—that is: being good and being bad—cannot be conceived as occasional attributes or properties that occur only during times of temptation or opportunity. To be is to be at risk. There is no special faculty such as our soul, conscience, spirit, or mind that provides us with these possibilities; rather, they come with our existence. To be is not only to be good or bad, it is to be good and bad. But this blurs the distinction between ethics and metaphysics. When we talk about the possibilities of being good and bad are we merely attributing freedom to the human person? Or is it the other way around? Perhaps being good and being bad is what makes the person possible at all. Perhaps good and bad make existence possible, and not the other way around. I take the "blurring" of the ethical-metaphysical to be an excellent thing for philosophy.

However we respond to such questions—and such response is the theme of the following chapter—there can be no doubt that our existence, once we have reached conscience and responsibility, is a risk. There is no avoidance; we cannot hide from it or disguise it for long without regret. It is part of our essential nature constantly to be at risk; for to be good is just as much a risk as to be bad. We are not "given substances" that on occasion have to decide—the good and the bad make us possible and provide us with possibilities. Otherwise possibilities would be meaningless. That to *feel* this is joy can be learned from Beethoven and Schiller. Now we must further learn how to *think* about it.

13

The Logos of Being Good

It is helpful now to restate the original question: What does it mean to be good? But this question can be amplified in two different ways:

1. What does it mean to be good or bad? or
2. What does it mean to be good and not be bad?

The first question asks for the metaphysical possibility of being able to be good or bad, often expressed in terms of freedom or agency. The question then becomes: how am I to understand this free agent or agency? Is there a special part or facility in us called the will? When I am faced with a moral decision and am tempted, who or what *explains* the way I make my judgment? If there are causes that account for this act, it seems, I am determined; if there is some noncausal and responsible agency, it would seem then I am free.

The second question seems to assume the first and asks what accounts for the moral strength or wisdom to do what is right. Or it may invite an entirely descriptive endeavor in which the thinker spells out in detail the difference between being good and being bad so as not only to inform the reader what these differences are but perhaps also to persuade the reader by this description that being good is preferable to being bad.

Or is there perhaps a third possibility, in which these two amplifications are seen as distractions from the primal truth of the original, unexpanded question? And if we do admit that all three possibilities deserve consideration, as perhaps they must, then the question would be which of these three formulations is the fundamental one? Which of these three, in other words, makes the other two possible?

The insistence throughout the inquiry that we are never wholly good or entirely bad, but that these opposing forces that make us who we are must always coexist, seems to give precedence to the first expanded version of the question. It is the "metaphysical" version of the question and appears therefore to outrank the others. But even if we assume this priority, the probing cannot resist further refinement. What is the difference between these two formulations of number 1?

1a: What does it mean to *be* good or bad?
1b: What does it mean *to be able* to be good or bad?

This multiplying of the ways to raise the question may seem comical in its delay of any response by always refining the divisions. But there is a serious problem here, for to ask about the ability to be good or bad (1b) seems to demand some pre-ethical, ontological question, as if "being good" is derived from some more fundamental notion, the way the meteorological accounts of the prevailing winds presuppose and depend upon the more basic principles of astronomy that explain the earth's rotation. So, just as astronomy is more fundamental than meteorology, so ontology is more fundamental than ethics.

Nevertheless, it does seem a little silly to skirt so dangerously near the endless regress inherent in this approach. What is to prohibit us from adding 1c: What does it mean to be able to be able to be good or bad? And, of course, once this is allowed there seems no need to stop, and we could go on down the alphabet, apparently each addition driving us to a deeper understanding. The conclusion would have to be that the method that allows for such regress is seriously flawed. The further troubling issue, whether ethics can

be "reduced" to metaphysics or ontology is likewise serious and
draws into question the validity of the method.

But this approach cannot be dismissed merely by threats of infinite regression or reductionism. The first amplification (1a) is in
fact defended by no less a titan in philosophy than Kant; and the
second refinement of this (1b) is defended by Heidegger. The issues
are therefore too serious to be so cavalierly tossed into the dustbin
of methodological amphibolies. But that such imminent and profound minds have seen fit to analyze these issues on such fundamental levels requires a more reverential approach.

What is asked in the first amplification (1a)? To be good *or* bad is
to focus on possibility and decision—possibility being here a metaphysical notion (both being good and being bad are genuine possibilities; the world is so designed as to allow either to occur, and
whichever does occur is consistent with all the metaphysical principles that explain the world.) Decision, however, is an ethical notion with metaphysical presuppositions: if I can choose (or decide)
between being good and being bad then *my* metaphysical nature
must be such as to allow for the ascription of responsibility; I must
be free. This seems to be Kant's view. As always, Kant asks: given
the fact that I can do something, such as mathematics, science, or
moral action, I must always ask *how* I can do it, and for Kant the
answer is always: a faculty. I can do mathematics because of the
faculty of the sensibility; I can do science because of the faculty of
the understanding; and I can do morally significant acts because
of the faculty of the (free) will. Thus the first amplification, "What
does it mean to be good *or* bad" is answered in Kant's terms: "Having a free will." But this is obviously too glib even for Kant. What is
it, Kant rightly asks, that makes a will good or bad? Have we not
merely put the dangerous instrument on a higher shelf out of the
reach of children? For we are no longer speaking of our doing good
things but of our *wills* doing good things. For Kant, the good will is
that which wills the adherence to the universal moral law. So, to *be*
good is to *will* the good. The will now becomes a faculty of the mind
that accounts for our doing things, just as being receptive to external stimuli is due to the faculty of the sensibility.

But what, one may ask, *accounts* for one man's willing well or
morally and another's willing ill or immorally? The answer cannot
be some other, deeper faculty, for *that* initiates an inevitable *reduc-*

tio ad absurdum. Kant seems to suggest that the will itself accounts for it. I will to do what is good because of my will. But this does not sound very helpful. We seem to be left with a fanciful description of rather common beliefs: Joe does bad things because he's bad; Pete does good things because he's good. There may be some obviousness in these simple remarks, but very little illumination. What is the difference—that is, the new information or insight—between "John is guilty of theft," and "John's will is guilty of theft?" Kant's answer, it seems, is that the term "will" here is merely a designation of the fact of responsibility. But then it is no longer a faculty. "The good will is that will that wills the good" may be consistent, but hardly helpful. Indeed, it may not be consistent at all; it may be an amphiboly, since "good" in the first usage may be subtly different than in the second. For surely the will does not will itself?

This in no way challenges Kant's account of the Categorical Imperative. It merely shows that there is at least a difficulty inherent in the notion of the "will." And it is precisely because of this that Heidegger, in an attempt to redeem Kant even as he surpasses Kant, opts for 1b: What does it mean *to be able* to be good or bad? In other words, do away with "will" altogether, and speak only of "being able to" or "possibility." Heidegger himself calls this "transcendence," which can, in these cases in which he is interpreting Kant, be read as the mode in which we are able to do or be something. In other words, we shift from a metaphysics of faculties (Kant) to an ontology of modes or ways of being (Heidegger). The attempt is to rid the philosophical lexicon of unwanted, metaphysical dead weight by eliminating almost sacred terms (substance, faculty, free will) because, when pressed, they have no meaning. Such riddance is not merely cosmetic, for the reliance upon unnecessary concepts to explain anything is always bad philosophy.

But even this account needs to be critically tested. Apparently I am good because I am able to be good. But this ability is likewise applicable to being bad. If we say "I am good because I am able to be good or bad" we have obviously made a profound point, since we have shifted from the language of faculties to the language of modalities, but the answer is still incomplete. For I do not want merely to know that I am *able* to do what is good, but how and why I select being good as preferable to being bad. Is it merely ignorance to choose the bad, as Socrates seems to suggest? Or is it some internal power or agency that accounts for it? But these accounts are regressive; they lead us right back to mysterious metaphysics where things happen because of precedent powers, and we know the powers are there because thing happen.

There is no doubt that to focus on the question of how we are able to be good or bad is a profound and necessary enterprise for the philosopher. But it cannot be fundamental, since too much is begged. Whether it is Kant or Heidegger, to say that a faculty or a mode of being precedes and accounts for our being good or bad in no way tells us what we want to know.

We can properly label this "being able to" as freedom, and say in quite ordinary language that to be able to be good or bad is simply the same thing as being free. But, although this is doubtlessly true, it neither shows that we are free, nor how to make sense of why one agent chooses the good and another the bad. It seems we are merely inventing technically obscure terms torturously to say what every child can say. Yet, as philosophers we cannot return to childish innocence or naiveté as if truth were imbedded in nostalgia. Nor should this discussion be seen as "refutations" of Kant or Heidegger, for their reasoning is far more subtle and far-reaching than this sketch suggests. We are asking a very specific question within a specific context: What is the rational structure that makes the question what is means to be good *thinkable?* This question is a natural follower of the prior chapter in which we asked not about the *thinkability* of being good (its logos) but the ability to *experience* the good (its pathos). But if the logos of the good relies either on the assumption of a faculty, the will, or even on a purely ontological notion such as having possibilities, the penetrating agitation and truth-provoking freshness of our question is lost or buried.

Perhaps, then, it is fitting now to focus on the second of the two amplifications. What does it mean to be good as opposed to bad? This formulation seems to avoid the rather dizzying spectacle of the ever-shrinking, perhaps even vanishing, power or agency that accounts metaphysically for our ability to be good, and returns us directly to the question of being good itself. In other words, we shift from asking by what *power* we can be good to what it *means* to be good. This question has the advantage of the support found in our

reflections on the three ways of being good discussed in the previous sections.

But surely, with this question, we cannot avoid the classical response: What it means to be good is to be happy. Why else *be* good
unless it makes us happy? Even the previous chapter shows that
joy is the pathos of goodness, so the eudaemonian must at least be
within the same general realm. But now it is even clearer why this
honored and traditional analysis fails. Happiness simply has too
many meanings. Specifically, and perhaps most important, it can
mean both a feeling (pathos) and a state or even a set of conditions. And when we mix these different meanings into the same
mode, nothing but confusion ensues. We ask, is it good to be
happy? The answer depends upon what sense is given to the various terms, for even unreflective people recognize that one who has
achieved happiness immorally does not deserve it, and hence is
not good. This then, is refined to say that "true" happiness or "real"
happiness cannot consist of ill-gotten delights, but only if the happiness of others is maintained. But the happiness of others—as
opposed to the pleasure of others—requires that each of the others
be brought to the same profound realization that "real" happiness
is making oneself and others happy. But this approaches circularity. What makes us happy is the "making us happy." Which is
it? Is it what makes us *feel* happy, or is it what actions *produce* the
feelings of happiness? If the eudaemonian insists that true happiness (as pathos) is the *making* of other's happiness (as a state or as
a condition), there is ambiguity. If the distinction is not made,
there is circularity.

We ask: Does being good make us happy? Obviously not, since
sacrifice is good but by definition it is the surrendering of something that makes us happy. Were the eudaemonian to insist that
sacrifice, though denying happiness as a direct pathos, nevertheless makes us happy in the sense of befitting the proper conditions
for being good, we then know he is simply being slick, for that argument is surely an amphiboly.

It is not my intention to become involved in disputes about conflicting and vying moral theories; it is rather an attempt to come to
grips with the simple but elusive title question of this chapter.
What is the logos of the good? That is, we are asking how we reason about what it means to be good (and not how we *feel* about

this question, for that is analyzed in the prior chapter). The present reflections show that a calculus of happiness cannot provide
us with the answer. But neither are we asking what the logos of
being *able* to be good is; for as we have seen, that directs us to a
series of mysterious entities such as wills and agents that do not
explain being good but rather themselves are explained by being
good. Perhaps it may be profitable to raise the question more na-
kedly. What, if anything, does being reasonable have to do with
being good?

This question is by no means as simple as it seems. The utilitarians perceive the good as achieving happiness for the most,
and reason's role is entirely calculative; indeed in some cases it is
purely quantitative, so that arithmetic is the essence of ethics.
Kant and other deontologists, however, argue quite otherwise: The
very nature of reason as universal is the guide to making moral
judgments, and the adherence to whatever law is inherent in such
universality determines our submission to it as an unquantifiable
duty. So *how* reason plays a role in making moral judgments becomes as dicey as arguing for any of the great ethical theories in
our history. Fortunately it is not necessary for this inquiry—asking
this specific form of the question—to dig into these ageless and
wonderful quarrels. For the entire persuasion of this approach is
to re-ask such great questions in terms of what it means to be
good, in part to show that such formulation is the most fundamental, and hence the truest way to raise the question.

Once again, however, it is necessary to refine the question by
considering different ways to address the problem. We ask:

3. Is being good reasonable? or
4. Is being reasonable good?

To pose the question in these two ways is deeply revealing, for we
note that if on the one hand we ask whether being good is reasonable (3) we are measuring the former by the latter: what counts is
being reasonable, and if being good qualifies, then it makes sense.
The great question of the entire inquiry would then be more easily
focused: What it means to be good is to be rational. This may seem
to reduce ethics to logic, which is at least a step above reducing it
to arithmetic; but in fact the formulation is far more richly con-

ceived than that. To say that what it means to be good is to be reasonable (or even "rational") seems almost irrefutable, since to argue for the position—or even to argue against it—is to say that the rationality of being good is inherent just in raising the question.

On the other hand, to focus on number 4 and ask if being reasonable is good measures reason by the standards of goodness. It is to ask *in what ways* being rational can qualify as being good, and this suggests there may be ways of being rational that are not good at all. Do we not attribute brilliance and cunning to the most diabolic offenders? Or, at the very least, do we not consider the logician as logician to be morally neutral? There seems to be no connection at all between being rational and being good, since many fine logicians can be either saint or sinner, and many saints may be fairly irrational in their behavior and perhaps even in their thinking.

But to ask if it is reasonable to be good is also to raise the possibility that the very foundation of all true reasoning rests on being able to be good. The question then becomes not how I can think about being good, as if being good were on a fairly long list of other things I can think about, but that the concern for being good within the preestablished conflict of being able to be good or bad, is the very basis of rationality itself; that being able to be good (and not: "or bad") establishes the very possibility of a certain kind of fundamental thinking, and perhaps even the very basis of all reasoning whatsoever.

This view of reasoning is sometimes called "ideality" and is often attributed to Plato and some of his earlier predecessors. According to this view, reason is our finite attempt to achieve a certain degree of self-realization that, when properly understood, is to be good. Thus reason is in the service of our nature as being able to be good and bad but striving always for the former. Reason, in other words, is always concerned with the achievement of our own excellence; but since we are finite—not in the sense of temporally limited but in the sense of being both good and bad—this achievement must be supplanted with mere achieving. Our temporal finitude *follows* from this achieving rather than the other way around. Such reasoning is so remarkable that it deserves our attention, not as a mere historical study of what Plato may or may not have meant, but on its own, as a possibility directly to be addressed.

What, after all, does it mean to reason? And we note here the superiority of this formulation or even translation—we do not ask: what is reason? Reasoning is what we do in the absence of direct apprehension of reality. We reason because we do not know. God does not reason. The notion that reason is our only perfect access to what is absolutely true is a misapprehension, due in part to a misunderstood passage in Aristotle's *Prior Analytics* that the syllogism gives us perfect knowledge. Logic, of course, does not give us truth, and hence not knowledge, but only validity, i.e., correctness of inferences. That Aristotle is aware of this is evidenced in his titling the books on logic as an *Organon;* that is, it is a tool. The function of this tool is very precise: it keeps us from contradiction. It cannot give us new knowledge. Aristotle's concept of *nous* is far richer than this, of course; but we are here speaking of reasoning in the syllogistic sense.

But if reason, even if broadened to the wider and richer senses of *nous*, is what we do because, unlike God, we do not directly apprehend the essence of things, including our own existence, then it must be seen as the fundamental attribute of our ontological (and not merely temporal) finitude. The nature of this finitude cannot be seen merely negatively; for we are no more completely ignorant than we are completely wise. Somehow being able to reason must be seen as that curious confrontation of our own moral finitude; i.e., being able to be good or bad.

We now see the significance of the analyses of the three ways of being bad and good. Judgment is neither perfect knowledge nor entirely subjective guessing; moral strength or weakness is neither total submission to any and all allure, nor is it the triumph over all resistance; character is that which grows and becomes, either in the direction of corruption or in the direction of excellence. But if this is what is meant by reasoning, then it is reasonable to be good (4) and not merely good to be reasonable (3). Being able to be good *and* bad (not: good *or* bad) is the basis of all reasoning whatsoever. For we do not reason merely to obtain knowledge, but to learn and become who we are.

As Heraclitus has discovered, the beginning of reason (as opposed to mere calculation) rests with the realization that all is in flux, including and especially ourselves. But for us to be in flux does not mean merely that we change in space and time, but that we succeed and fail to achieve our own excellence. In varying from state to state or moment to moment I am no different than a pig or a leaf. What is in flux for us is the difference between being good and bad. This difference forces us to reflect on who we are, which is the beginning of true thinking. Hence, it is not reason that measures goodness but goodness that measures reason.

But these arguments, though fascinating, require some precising of definitions; for what is meant by the differences between thinking, reasoning, being conscious, and calculating? To calculate is to figure out the taxonomy of things, to put things together so that they fit into a broader framework without contradiction, and to distinguish cause from effect. To reason is that subspecies of thinking that provides authority. It is, if you will, thinking authoritatively. To be conscious is to be open to the impact of external stimuli and to be aware of one's own internal thoughts or ideas. Thinking is more than consciousness and calculation; though consciousness is formally fundamental because thinking, reasoning, and calculating all presuppose it and can be understood (cautiously) as kinds or ways of being conscious. To think, however, is the noblest of these, for in thinking we rank and synthesize all of the others, and we reflect on our own meaning. It is to allow truth to manifest itself and be recognized; it is therefore both active and passive, and its chief concern is its own truth, both in *letting* truth *happen* and in probing or seeking truth as a boon.

With these brief accounts—they are too imprecise to be called definitions—we are now prepared to ask the title question of this chapter more precisely. If reasoning is authoritative thinking, whence comes this authority? What does it *mean* to *think* with authority? To put the question in this way prepares the answer that has been hinted at throughout these reflections; the fundamental authority lies in what it means to be good. There is authority only because truth about our own being matters. There is authority, and not merely success, because as finite, what it means to be good is manifested in judgment, moral strength, and nobility of character. For authority is not the same as success; it gives us the right and the power to do something, but not the guarantee.

This is not an essay in epistemology, so it is not the place to show how such thinking is done. But this chapter's title question can now be provisionally answered: the logos of the good is idealization. However, in arriving at this characterization, we have also unearthed the possibility that being good and bad is the fundamental authority for all thought. How can thus be?

We recall that Kant argues that the authority behind the Categorical Imperative—that which makes it a law before which we all must be in awe—is the very nature of reason itself as universal. But surely it is the other way around. It is precisely because the moral law is a guide that directs us to be good that we recognize its universality. It is not the universality (or "rationality") that makes it good, but our own being able to be good that establishes its universality or rationality. Formally, of course, the Kantian argument is correct; but existentially it is its inversion that matters. In the prior account of character as noble it was shown that in being good we also reflect as a mirror the universal meaning of goodness, making each man, as good, a model for the world and himself. This is a kind of existential universality that is concretely more fundamental than the formal universality of Kant. To idealize is to mirror or reflect what it means to be good, and this is what gives it authority. The logos of being good is the authority inherent in this mirroring; it is idealization, the supreme ground of all reasoning whatsoever.

We speak here not of the authority of the moral law, as Kant does, but of the authority in being good. The power of judgment, courage, and character to *illuminate* what it means to be good is founded on the authority inherent in being good. But to reason thus is to think with authority; indeed it is concretely to confront our own truth with authority (though not with guarantee.) Since we define reasoning as thinking with authority, to be able to be good, and hence to mirror or reflect authority, makes idealization, and perhaps other forms of reasoning, possible. This is the logos of being good.

In this chapter we have made a goodly number of subtle re-formulations of the original question. Which takes precedence? It should be obvious now that it is the original formulation that outranks all others. This is true not only because it is the origin of the others, and to some extents contains them, but because the original formulation asks something that none of the others can. Why is this question, "what does it mean to be good?" more fundamental than how we ought to act or how should we live our lives or whether we possess freedom or by what power or faculty do we choose? These few final reflections may serve as an indicator.

Why should I obey these laws, assuming I believe them to be the proper moral precepts? Because I want to be good. Why do I weigh this ethical system with that ethical system? Because in judging rightly about which is correct, I not only care about the truth, but also about being good. Were someone to show me that my previous ethical beliefs were wrong, and that a new code were correct, what I understand by "wrong" is that the first code will not help me to be good, whereas the new set of precepts will show me how to be good. Even if I base my moral thinking on consequences and utility, the reasoning is the same, though more weakly supported. If I am shown that my previous conduct has bad consequences I shall alter them, not merely to avoid bad consequences but because in having (or producing) good consequences I can esteem myself as *being* good. Thus, what it means to be good is always the ultimate, underlying, and final concern of moral and ethical thinking. There is no good reason not be address this question directly.

But why should the form of the question be couched in terms of "meaning" and "being"? What does it mean to *ask* such a thing? Why not ask what it means to *do* good? Or why not ask what the concept of good is or even The Good? The fundamental question is raised in terms of "being" and "meaning" because, as fundamental, this question directs the inquiry to the *reality* of being good. The final chapter, therefore, focuses briefly but precisely on this point.

14

The Reality of Being Good

The Metaphysics of Being Good

This title is carefully chosen; it is not "the reality of the good," as if goodness were some kind of entity or, worse, abstraction. Entities, including events, can be said to exist, but existence is not all there is to being. To be real—and this is the proper way to address "reality"—is to be the basis of truth and meaning. Honor and justice may be real—which means they may also possibly be illusory—but they do not exist. Manifestations of them may exist and events that may be characterized as honorable or just may exist or happen, but to speak of their reality cannot lead us to the invalid inference that they exist as objects in the world. This care taken in the precising of the terminology initiates this final chapter because the danger of misinterpretation here is greater. The attacks on a substantive metaphysics begun by Hume and Kant and raised to powerful insight by Heidegger are well known but often overlooked or simply disregarded. To say that for an entity to exist it must be the object of actual or possible experience, as Kant argues, is to limit the range of existence but not to equate it with reality, which is a broader notion. But reality and existence can both be said to be or, more important, we can ask what it means to be real or to be an entity, and this makes *being* the broadest and most inclusive of the three major ontological terms. Since being cannot be limited either to existence or reality, it cannot be the object of experience nor articulated in terms of abstractions; hence, it must always and only be approached in terms of its meaning. Thus we ask what it means to be—to be this kind of thing, or to be in this mode or way, or to be as finite or infinite, or even what it means just to be at all.

To raise the very question of what it means to be already exposes something about us the questioners: Since we must *ask,* we are not directly and intuitively certain and, hence, we are finite. Upon reflection, indeed, this finitude is the most fundamental way in which the meaning of our being as reality can be approached. We are, in essence, finite or limited. To be limited itself has limits; i.e., we are not absolutely limited, but only in certain ways, else we could not think about our own meaning, nor could we even *be* meaningful.

There are four ways we are limited. The first has already been exposed by our asking the question: We are not possessed of infinite knowledge but neither are we unburdened by being totally ignorant. We are also limited in time, which does not merely mean we are going to die, but that our very being is in truth a becoming. We are in flux not merely as a flowering bush is always on its way either to full bloom or decay but self-consciously as we realize that we are unfolding as a story, ever learning who we are becoming. The third way of our finitude is spatial: We belong. We are neither ubiquitous nor do we coexist with the vastness of the world. We have a place, yet we ever widen and expand the place we belong as well as the places we do not belong. So the limits of time reveal that in essence we *become;* the limits of space reveal that in essence we *belong;* the limits of our knowledge show that in essence we *judge.*

But there is a fourth kind of limitation to our being: We are good and bad. This can only be called the risk of being, which is our reality. We are limited in our very reality not by time, space, or ignorance merely, but even more fundamentally by what we make of ourselves given our becoming, our belonging, and our judging. That I can be said *to be* good and bad, and not merely to *do* what is good and bad is to reveal the most profound of all the senses of being finite.

At the onset of this inquiry we examined the pathoempirical

truth of outrage, and in this examination we saw the curious and paradoxical risk that is inherent in this reaction to the wrongdoing of others. The phenomenon of outrage discloses not only the noble, universally valid demand to redress a wrong, but also the impotence, frustration, and agonizing loss of the precious, which is absolute and unredeemable. The very phenomenon that reveals our total loss—and hence our impotence—also generates the unlimited authority of justice. But that we are impotent in the very face of this authority is to be at risk; that is, being at risk is a mode of being finite. The risk is not that of possibly suffering bad or punitive consequences, nor is it a triumph of the daring over the stolid. Nor is it my own personal risk, but the risk of being itself.

We have seen that in judging well, which is the first way to be good, there is achieved a kind of coherence or synthesis of disparate elements. We "read" the shards and pieces as a mosaic, and hence become wise rather than foolish. In moral strength there is the resistance to disintegration, a holding fast to the whole and the solid, in which the strengthening is a congealing of those spiritual elements that would be dissipated in weakness. And in noble character, there is the wholeness or soundness of integrity, a sequestering of the precious that makes us unique even as it mirrors the whole as a model or paradigm. Thus the three ways of being good all share the common element of moral synthesis, of maintaining a unity that binds together. To be good is to be whole.

This good wholeness, however, can never be automatic or inherent; it is a wholeness always in the face of disintegration, an alluring, charming, pleasant sundering of the bonds until the gleeful shattering is in full counter to the joyous bonding. To be good relies on our being both good and bad: it is the confrontation with, and the on-going triumph over the bad. Thus the naive approach of Chapter 1, which is to see being good merely as not doing what is bad, like all naiveté, poorly reflects a profound truth. In a paradoxical way, we can be good only because we are bad, which is simply to say we are finite in both. But this insistence on the pervasive conflict between being good and being bad is not merely an appeal to ethical realism; nor is it a mere exercise of skeptical or cautionary suspicion. It is fundamental to our metaphysical essence as finite; that is, to our reality as finite.

What we identify as space and time in our experience of the external world is, when directed ontologically on our own reality, belonging and becoming. We belong and we become—the union of these is what it means for us to be real. But to speak of belonging as a way of being good is to focus on unity in a communal and reverential sense: it is to be pious. This is not the same as being "pietistic," which is merely a quality of one's demeanor—the dour, rigid, unsmiling sternness and self-indulgent solemnity that is often puritanical and, equally often, bad. Piety, after all, is the formal condition for joy as the pathos of the good. It is also the ultimate presupposition for personal integrity. To be pious is simply to belong in a good way. This does not triumph the gregarious over the subdued; it is to take joy in the belonging that is part of our reality. Alienation or self-centered arrogance may often take the form of the socially active gladhander who cannot abide his own company but whose outgoing and noisy membership in groups manifests his disdain for true belonging. True piety takes joy in one's metaphysical spatiality: belonging.

If piety is the goodness of belonging, then what is the goodness of our becoming? This is learning; but it is a learning to become who we are, and is hence more than merely formal learning or the achievement of knowledge. We learn as we become and as we belong. But false learning can be bad, for we can grow alien to our belonging and indeed even distant from our reality. Ideology is often a form of educational alienation, for it is a species of retardation, in which we allow a set of doctrines or a "movement" to dictate for us all our behavior. Such communal submission is exactly the opposite of true belonging and hence personal integrity; and in terms of education, it is opposed to true becoming. It is possible, I suppose, to distinguish true learning, both from indoctrination and the mere achievement of information. To learn in the truest sense is to become who we are.

These metaphysical translations should not distract us from the integrity of the present inquiry, but they obviously deserve further treatment, and I have already initiated a subsequent volume to address these confrontational metaphysics more directly. It is enough, however, in the present context merely to show that what it means to be good is in fact metaphysically grounded in what it means to be at all, without any need for intermediate faculties or substances such as wills, agencies, or internal powers. In the last analysis, it is always and only *we* who are good and bad; and remarkably, the pronoun suffices. Indeed it is when the pronoun is given some substantive referent that the metaphysical fog rolls in, blinding us to our own moral reality. The pronoun is philosophically prior to and even superior to the noun, for it is a form of concrete universality even as it is immediate and directly meaningful. "I think, therefore I am," cannot be substituted by "Descartes thinks, therefore he is." We are good and bad, and this pronoun is not constructed from a plurality of "I's" nor need it be referentially designated in order to be meaningful. Above all, the claim that we are good and bad cannot be further reduced to wills or agents. All of these distractions diminish the authority and consequently the reality of being good and bad.

The Ethics of Being

To speak of the reality of being good and being bad cannot be covered merely by these metaphysical speculations, however. For the question of the reality of being good and bad is often raised in a more seriously ethical way. We seem to want to know if such notions are illusory, or culturally determined, or relativistic. We want to know whether we are fundamentally good, so that being bad is the result of alien institutionalization, or whether we are fundamentally bad, and the achievement of goodness is due to contractual origins of society or perhaps even the grace or bestowal of a forgiving and beneficent God. Are we *really* good? That is, are we *in reality* good? Or are we really bad?

In order to address these issues in light of the foregoing analyses, it may be helpful to ask a somewhat different question that is perhaps less speculative but more concrete. We ask: What is the greatest evil? This is obviously a companion question to that asked in Chapter 10, that raised the problem of the most troubling moral question. To ask what the greatest evil is does not ask for that action that brings about the greatest pain or suffering, nor does it ask which action deserves the most punishment. It is a reflective question, and hence the answer can only be given in terms of reflection.

The greatest evil is to deny its reality.

This truth is most clearly revealed on the sociopolitical realm. Naive claims to the effect that we, especially in our youth, are naturally good leads to disastrous social and political enactments and maxims that haunt history and our present culture. The will to be deceived by this naiveté leads Chamberlain to sign the Munich agreement with Hitler; national agencies to treat all criminals as victims of social ills such as poverty, drugs, and racism; excusing indolence and rebellion on the grounds of deprivation or unenlightenment. With the wringing of hands and the clucking of tongues we lament the gross decrease of cultural stability without taking punitive steps to control depravity. Some shake their heads and ask, as if it were a great mystery, why we go to war, never admitting the obvious answer that armies are needed primarily because there are genuinely wicked men whose cruelty, meanness, and tyranny must be stopped with force. Children are denied their greatest gift, childhood itself, by stupidly and, hence, wickedly pretending they are adults, and indeed naturally good ones at that. The social disasters that follow from these odious maxims are worse than the suffering imposed by evil men, since they leave us without identifiable enemies to recognize and fight against. This chilling romanticism so enervates the heroic that time after time we convince ourselves once again to put our hands on the hot stove, and recoil in anguish at being badly burned over and over. There are bad men, bad women, bad children, and bad institutions, and the denial of this wickedness is simply the greatest evil possible.

But this truth is even more insidious when it occurs within our own souls. There is an almost spectacular self-deception inherent in the denial of our own wickedness, as if all our faults come from forces outside ourselves. We rest contentedly within the warm convenience of our own assumed and natural goodness. In the analysis of temptation we have seen how the phenomenology of this submission corrupts, yielding a depredation so deeply entrenched that we become total slaves to our own blindness, a state of wretchedness made all the more defeating since to counter it we need only to open our eyes.

The most wretched state possible for us to be in is self-hatred. When we despise our own culture, loathe our own society, and detest our own existence we have reached the condition of absolute corruption. And yet it is this very wretchedness that we ourselves bring about as soon as we deny the reality of our own being able to be bad. Species-hatred is an inevitable consequence of this, when all we can see is our own pollution, our own misery, our own self-contempt. There are even some who look upon the beasts as our betters, not in moments of enlightened self-appraisal, but in actual loathing of our own humanity. There is nothing humble or salva-tory in this; it is simply disgusting, even pitiable. But its origin is in the naive view that we ought, by nature, to be blessed with un-troubled innocence. To be innocent is to be unable to be good be-cause we cannot be bad. It is not innocence that redeems but be-ing good, which requires a confrontation and struggling mastery with our own being bad.

The question whether we are fundamentally good or bad permits of only one of four possible answers:

1. We are basically good.
2. We are basically bad.
3. We are neither good nor bad.
4. We are both good and bad.

There is no doubt that we are often compelled to affirm the first answer. A father huddles protectively around his child as they slide together down the snowy hill, his heart aching with love both tender and necessary. Two young people lie on the grass in a ne-glected meadow, the spring sweetness of the flowers and the gentle whisper of a caressing breeze prompt their first touching; and they, of an instant, realize they shall never be the same again; and the realization of it, and they themselves, are now wonderful. The lonely woman is unexpectedly visited by concerned acquaintances who turn out miraculously to be and always have been her friends; and her gratitude is radiant in her smile. Are these not good things? We know that people are good, we resent the framed screens in our living room depicting only crime, suffering, war, or goodness embedded only in stupidity. The instances of human kindness are ubiquitous, and doomsayers, puritans, ascetics, and scolders seem never to have seen a child smile or a Shakespeare comedy or hear a Mozart piano concerto.

Yet the wickedness is there, too; and we are fools to deny it. But which is fundamental? Perhaps we are neither essentially good nor bad, but achieve these qualities by nonessential attribution. We can be good or bad, it seems, precisely because in our essence we are neutral. The moral attributes are not fundamental, but accidental in the Cartesian sense of that term. It would seem that the very changes that occur in a single life or in a single nation show that the moral qualities cannot be of our essence. How else do we explain the converted sinner becoming a saint, the reformed criminal becoming a good citizen, or the once merry child becoming a hardened prostitute? Who we are is one thing; that we become good or bad is quite another. Or it may be that some are born good and others born bad; but it cannot be that the species itself is all one or all the other just because there are both saints and sinners.

And yet, as persuasive as each of these arguments may seem, the only answer that can stand the test of critical analysis is the fourth option: we are essentially both good and bad. To be self-reflective is to be both good and bad in the very essence of what it means to be self-reflective. We are not sometimes good and at other times bad; nor are some of us naturally good and others naturally bad. We are not essentially good but fall away, nor are we essentially bad and heroically overcome our own evil nature. Rather we are essentially good *and* bad, always. The difference is in the achieved triumph, or perhaps even in the on-going struggle, down to the last, exhausted gasp, and starting from the first childhood discovery that temptation is both resistance and allure. It is of critical importance to realize this; for only in this realization can we confront the title question truthfully. We are not good *or* bad; we are good *and* bad.

The Greatest Good

If we can ask what the greatest evil is, surely we can also ask what the greatest good is. We are fortunate to have in our literature a brilliant and fascinating quarrel on how to approach this issue between two of the truly great thinkers in our tradition. Arthur Schopenhauer takes his admired predecessor, Immanuel Kant, severely to task in an almost comical rage, as found in the lengthy

appendix to *The World as Will and Representation*. The essence of
the quarrel is this. Kant gives an example of two wealthy men, both
of whom donate a considerable sum to the poor. The first is a
snobby aristocrat who disdains the great unwashed, and contemp-
tuously avoids their company. However, his reason convinces him
it is his duty to support the less favored of society, which leads him
to hire a financial expert to calculate exactly how much he ought to
pay; and once this figure is determined he writes a check to an
agent, unwilling even to descend to the unsavory hovels of his reluctantly endowed beneficiaries. The second man, of equal wealth
with the first, has a naturally warm and generous nature; he loves
his fellowman regardless of his station, and cheerfully dispenses
his generosity personally, taking joy in the delight he spreads
throughout the wanton and squalid streets of the deprived. Both
men give the same amount to the poor; but which of the two, Kant
asks, is morally superior? Is it the reluctant miser who yields only
because it is his duty, or the gracious benefactor rejoicing in his
kindness and generosity?

Kant claims the first is morally superior to the second; a judgment that seems to provoke in Schopenhauer a billingsgate of outrage, insult, and contempt upon the venerable sage of Königsberg.
How, Schopenhauer asks, could Kant be so cold and formal as to
miss the true nature of generosity? The second man is surely a
nicer fellow than the first, whose mean-spiritedness seems almost
to negate the goodness of his charity. This initiates the lively and
entertaining debate that is itself almost as enjoyable as a sporting
event, if for no other reason than the literary eloquence of Schopenhauer's incomparable style. But it is the reasoning that matters; and it is in the context of their conflicting argumentation that
so much valuable insight is learned.

Schopenhauer's argument at first sounds almost Kantian, as if
he were trying to out-Kant Kant. What matters, he claims is not
what you do but *why* you do it. Love is superior to calculation, the
character is more important than his action. By Kant's own reasoning then, and by the details of his own story, the second man is
much nicer than the first, he possesses true virtue, generosity, and
perhaps even love, and he does his duty as well. To prefer the first
man is a suggestion so bereft of any admirable sentiment or passion as to indict the agent of all moral quality whatsoever. To some

extent, of course, this quarrel is entirely unequal, since Schopen-hauer is one of the great stylists of the German language, whereas Kant is usually, though not always, turgid, dry, tedious and Prussian. But Schopenhauer's deepest argument is that reason itself is not the origin or even the protector of morality; rather it is resistance to the world will that makes the saint. This resistance sets up a counter-will to the world-will, which it embodies in character; and character is achieved independently of the Principle of Sufficient Reason.

The Kantian response to this, of course, is that the naturally generous bestower is doing what he likes to do. His actions are admittedly good deeds, but he does them because he takes pleasure in them. It is far more admirable, surely, to do one's duty simply because it is right, and not because we just *happen* to want to do what we ought. Let us press the analogy: suppose I take delight in not doing my duty? Is it a matter of sheer inclination? Are the good merely lucky in having the right genes? The entire suasion of Kant's analysis is that we cannot rely upon these pleasant inclinations precisely because some may be beneficent and others wicked. To rely upon the power and strength of the only faculty that is *not* controlled by sentiment, namely reason, is what true courage really means. Surely it is sounder to trust the man who submits only to the authority of his mind. A southern American growing up in the first half of the twentieth century may have been taught to believe and feel that Blacks were inferior; but if his own reasoning compels him reluctantly to admit the inherent dignity of all men, his respect for whom he once despised and for whom even yet feels an inherited unfriendliness, is all the more spectacular because of the triumph of what is right over what is felt. One may call this "unfeeling," and in a way, of course, it is—but only because not all feelings are trustworthy.

This magnificent dispute will probably never be settled, for the arguments on both sides seem so attractive. The dispute need not be raised in terms of Kant and Schopenhauer, who have merely lifted it to the level of the sublime. But even everyday, ordinary folk confront this issue and find it vexing. Respect for law is so fundamental and so necessary that violations of it simply cannot be tolerated; yet a concern for an individual's privacy and belonging is also too precious to be abandoned. Are not forgiveness and mercy, as Portia instructs us, also a part of us? Merely to obey laws without concern for feelings may make us into mere machines; but disregard for the authority of law may make us into beasts. But is it not better to be a beast than a machine? At least a beast has a heart. The deep anguish of this question is nowhere more splendidly revealed than in Herman Melville's short novel *Billy Budd*, where the innocent and beloved Billy is caught up in a legal violation that seems to require the honor-bound Captain Vere to pass the dread sentence of death on the hapless boy he knows to be good. So painful is this confrontation that we realize we are burdened unfairly with judgments we have no right to make but whose disregard is even more horrible to contemplate. We beg to be excused, for these burdens simply are beyond our powers. But we are denied. We simply must judge even when, as finite, our judgment must be flawed. Is there greater anguish than this? It seems that in asking for what is the greatest good we have instead produced the greatest anguish. Is there a cruel but brilliant lesson here? Is this bitter dose perhaps medicinal?

The dispute between Kant and Schopenhauer may not be resolvable in the sense that one side must concede all its authority, but its vexation can, and indeed must, be muted; for there is a false dichotomy here. Kant is asking a moral question, Schopenhauer an ethical one. Both are more right than they are wrong; and where they are wrong is in the extent or range given to their claims. Kant is entirely correct that duty is absolute, and that no mere sentiment can outweigh its authority. Schopenhauer is correct in attributing ethical goodness to character that is not reducible to the Principle of Sufficient Reason. Both offend by denying any authority to the other, which is to say that both offend by taking an overly narrow view of what is good. Both also offend, on a most human and most forgivable level, in seeking to remove the anguish that comes from not resolving the clash between ethical goodness and moral goodness. Both would rid the beleaguered Captain Vere of his bitter judgment, and in this, both are wrong. For Vere would not be Vere without it.

It is therefore not by accident that in seeking out the greatest good we uncover the greatest anguish. For perhaps it is not love, nor happiness, nor duty, nor obedience, nor reason, nor character that is the greatest good, but it is in the embrace and confrontation of the very anguish that seems to tear us apart. When we realize the dire need to judge with insufficient capacity, and accept this wholly unnatural burden on ourselves because this is who we are, we conjoin the ethical and the moral under an existential confrontation and find in it that which is the greatest good because it is as good as we can get.

If indeed the greatest evil is to deny that there can be evil perhaps it is the greatest good to accept and even embrace with passion the terrible truth that there be both good and evil. This is to conjoin courage with love; it is at once the most rigorously adherent to law and yet the most passionate acceptance of our vulnerability and need for measured mercy. We ally ethical goodness with moral right under the hegemony of ethical truth, and discover that the confrontation of the bad is supremely good. So it is not merely that we must be satisfied with the grudging crumb we finite spaniels are thrown from the tables of gods, but that the truth of being good is far more precious and radiant than what ethics or morality, or even both combined, can offer.

To mention the gods here is to suggest an amplification of an idea first raised in Chapter 1. To ask if God exists or is real of course presupposes first that we have some idea of what it means for there to be a God. I cannot asks whether a tump exists, for I do not know what a tump is. These reflections on what it means to be good have broken the sod in a virgin field. If we entertain our inheritance to the extent that God must be good by definition, whether he be real or no, we now can dig and plant into this new ground or essence, and see if the soil is fruitful. God, as the supreme reality, would be defined as that being for whom the greatest evil is his greatest possibility, resisted. Loving creation is thus the risky difference between being good and being bad in the ongoing conflict; an unending struggle of the absolutely mighty between an evil whose perfection is its self-denial, and a goodness whose perfection is its self-embrace. This may seem the grossest kind of anthropomorphism, making the infinite intelligible by making it finite. But this accusation rests upon the faulty premise that has beguiled all theodicists and atheists who reject God because of evil, that to be good is possible without being bad; and that the supremely good is to be entirely free of even the possibility of being bad. The theodicist theologian does not allow God to be good. What these arguments show is exactly the opposite. If to be good is to confront and hence limit the bad without removing its possibility, then one who is absolutely good would be one who contends with the greatest possible evil, an evil that must always be present, not as a mere possibility, but as an imminent, real threat, kept at bay only by the tiniest advantage inherent in absolute might, the power and authority of which just *is* this narrow triumphing of the continual battle of titans called "being good."

Some may protest that this anthropomorphic language is misleading; that to define God as one whose greatest possibility is the greatest evil, suffices; that to talk about struggles and might and triumph is to give a philosophically sophisticated analysis an entirely inappropriate flavoring of myth, mysticism and monsters. But it seems that exactly the opposite danger is the true threat; that language so formalized as to be nothing but a topography of necessary and sufficient conditions threatens to become entirely meaningless. For the origin here is our own being good and bad. This is a concrete, testable and meaningful beginning that has been analyzed with considerable fruition. We now are testing these discoveries, these truths, on one of the most fretful and vexations of human reflections: whether being good and bad is compatible with theistic belief. It is not at all an argument for God's reality, but an argument about what it must mean for there to be a God. To pre-empt this attempt on the grounds that the language is concrete seems retrograde to the inquiry as well as to the emerging truth.

Such a God, of course, would be closer to that loved by the saint than that anatomized by the theologian; one approached more closely by the worshipper than the orthodox; though it may skirt some ancient heresies to the effect that in bringing God and man closer together it defeats the absolute transcendence of the divine. But the logic here favors the passions: if God be good, he cannot so transcend the meaning of the term "good" as to be thought merely in terms of innocence. These transcendent theologians in fact do not make God good but innocent, indeed absolutely and supremely innocent—and hence incapable of being good. For we know what it means to be good; and we know what the greatest evil and the greatest good are: to deny evil is the greatest evil; to embrace being both good and bad is the greatest good. To claim God is good is thus to deny he is innocent. To say God is absolutely good is to say he narrowly, but decisively, triumphs over the greatest possible evil. Dostoyevsky's account of Christ's temptation in the desert echoes this awesome, existential truth, for the great temptation of Christ was that by miracle he makes being bad impossible. That would be the worst of all possible worlds—though every utopian and theodicist and atheist sees it otherwise—for in such a world we could not *be good.*

This final detour into the speculative dangers of theodicy is not meant as a new theological discovery. Rather, these reflections are of the entire inquiry itself; they mirror, as all idealizing should, a truth that can only be approached through mirroring. Arguments about the existence or non-existence of God are here superfluous. It is not God's goodness but our own being good that matters first. From outrage and judgment, to character and joy, the plow has unearthed its ground, and the risk of being has been upended from the darkness and broken through the light. If nothing else we know we can think about what it means to be good, and the truth of it matters absolutely.

Michael Gelven is Professor of Philosophy at Northern Illinois University and the author of several books, including *A Commentary on Heidegger's* Being and Time (Harper & Row, 1970; rev. ed., Northern Illinois University Press, 1989), *Spirit and Existence* (University of Notre Dame Press, 1990), *Truth and Existence* (Penn State Press, 1990), *Why Me? A Philosophical Inquiry into Fate* (Northern Illinois University Press, 1991), *War and Existence* (Penn State Press, 1993), and *The Quest for the Fine: Judgment, Worth, and Existence* (Rowman and Littlefield, 1996).